Clathrate Inclusion Compounds

SISTER *Mary* MARTINETTE HAGAN, *1910-*
Department of Chemistry
Mundelein College
Chicago

New York
REINHOLD PUBLISHING CORPORATION
Chapman & Hall, Ltd., London

A.M.D.G.

Foreword

The fact that quinol and sulfur dioxide unite to form a stable, crystalline compound was discovered three quarters of a century ago, but the elucidation of the true nature of this and similar substances is a discovery of very recent times. Indeed, the word "clathrate" was coined to describe them only thirteen years ago. The subsequent history of these remarkable materials is not only of great scientific interest, but it serves as an exciting example of the far reaching results which fundamental research can produce. The clathrate compounds were little more than chemical curiosities until the x-ray studies of Palin and Powell revealed their structure; this discovery suggested the possibility that they might be used in effecting separations of closely related substances, and many such applications were quickly developed. More recently, this same knowledge of structure has led to the use of clathrates as catalysts, stabilizing agents, and anti-oxidants, and there is evidence that clathrate formation plays an important role in biological processes. At the same time, continued fundamental research on the clathrates has added to our knowledge of the mode of formation of crystals and the magnitude of crystal forces. As chemists learn to synthesize clathrates with specific and special properties, new concepts and new applications will surely be discovered.

In this excellent review of the current status of our knowledge of the clathrate compounds, Sister Mary Martinette has collected information which will be helpful to both students and research workers. They will find here, not only answers to their questions about the structure, properties, synthesis and uses of the clathrates, but also many suggestions for further research. It is a book that deserves wide and careful study.

May 1, 1962   JOHN C. BAILAR, JR.

Preface

Clathrates are complex compounds composed of two or more components. They differ from other complex compounds in that the molecules of their components are associated without ordinary chemical bonding. In each case there is complete enclosure of the molecules of one component in a suitable structure which has been formed by the molecules of the other. Clathrate compounds are now emerging on the chemical scene to take a place of increasing importance. Their formation is novel, and their properties are unique. When forming they appear to disdain the normal types of bonding and seldom do they fall into strictly inorganic or organic classifications. Though they are similar to inclusion compounds, in fact are a type of inclusion compound, clathrates are generally more thorough in their inclusion propensities.

The existence of such compounds was recorded as early as 1886 when Mylius[175] observed interesting and intriguing features in the complex compounds formed by hydroquinone with certain volatile substances. He suggested that no ordinary combination occurred between the molecules which formed the complexes, and that in some way the molecules of one component were able to lock the molecules of the second component into position, but without chemical bonding. To him it seemed probable that a complex resulted from the complete enclosure of one molecule by two or more molecules of another component in such a manner as to prevent escape of the enclosed molecule, unless the strong forces which bound together the enclosing molecules could be broken.

Stimulation of interest in this unusual behavior was reawakened by the work of Palin and Powell[186] who, over sixty years later, verified the results of Mylius by means of very accurate x-ray studies. They found that hydroquinone molecules link together through hydrogen bonds to form infinite three-dimensional complexes and that these giant molecules will, indeed, enclose a second component. Powell and co-workers observed and grouped together the characteristics which compounds of this type have in common[200—227,305]. They observed the firmness with which the components of clathrates were held together even though no strong attractive forces appeared to be acting between them; that the components were held together in the compound by the enclosure of one by the other, of both by each other, or by some uncommon mechanism. Because of the unusual type of binding which he noted, Powell proposed that the compounds be called "clathrate" compounds, from the Latin word *clathratus* meaning enclosed or protected by cross bars of a grating[204].

Although a careful study of representative types of clathrate compounds is necessary for a workable understanding of their nature, a few generalizations and observations will serve to introduce the more compre-

hensive presentation. From the very beginning of the
work on these compounds it was quite apparent that
considerations of size and of type of bonding within the
cage-like component would enter into an understanding of their nature. Common sense dictates that the
form, which the molecular aggregates of the first component of such enclosures takes, will have to contain
spaces of size great enough to hold a molecule of the
second component. Also, that the spaces will have to
be bound in such a manner as to prohibit escape of the
enclosed molecules. It seems likely that, when formation takes place, the molecules to be enclosed will have
to be properly oriented when the cage closes. When a
cavity forms without enclosing a molecule of the second component, the difficulty of getting one in is
expected to be equal to that of getting one out. Each
of these characteristics is observed. It is noted, too,
that molecules can, and do, escape from within the
cages.

Each new observation eventually sets into motion
studies on appropriate applications of these characteristics. Meanwhile, fundamental research on such
properties as structure, behavior in solution, magnetic
susceptibilities, and many others, continue to add
steadily to the accumulation of information on clathrate compounds.

To acquaint its readers with clathrates and their
behavior is the purpose of this book. In order to do
this the place of clathrates in the hierarchy of compounds is first established. Molecular compounds are
discussed initially because clathrates are molecular

compounds. In Ch. 1 the nature, classification, and behavior of molecular compounds in general, and from the viewpoint of several authors, are set forth. This is done very briefly. Next, a subdivision of molecular compounds known as inclusion compounds is singled out for special inspection because clathrates are inclusion compounds. Clathrates, however, are only one type of inclusion compound; therefore it is necessary to point out what inclusion compounds are, what kinds of inclusion compounds there are, how they resemble one another, and how they differ from one another. With this task completed in Ch. 1, the remainder of the book is given over to a discussion of the various aspects of the nature and uses of clathrate compounds.

Rare, indeed, is the author who is not indebted to many colleagues. In this instance the author wishes to acknowledge the invaluable assistance of Dr. B. Peter Block, Professor Bodie Douglas, and Professor J. V. Quagliano who read the manuscript critically and made numerous helpful suggestions. An expression of gratitude is sincerely offered to Professor John C. Bailar, Jr., teacher and friend, for his interest and encouragement. Several points regarding clathrate compounds were clarified by Professor H. M. Powell of Oxford University, England, who kindly supplied many reprints and discussed his work with the author.

The author is grateful for the encouragement of her colleagues at Marillac College where she has been Visiting Chemistry Professor for the past three years, and for that of her Mundelein College colleagues, Sisters of Charity, B.V.M. The assistance of Sister

Mary Bartella, B.V.M. and of Miss Irene Hojnacki in typing the final copy, and that of Mr. George Kleine, Jr., the artist, is sincerely appreciated.

Permission to select data freely and to reproduce illustrations from the publications of the American Chemical Society, from *Nucleonics*, and from several of the many authors whose papers are listed in the References has made this book possible. The references which have been given are those which seemed most pertinent. Of necessity, many excellent papers have been treated very sketchily. The task of writing the book seemed at first glance easier than it actually was. The unfailing and friendly responses to requests for reprints and information, as well as the proffered assistance of many colleagues, contributed to the author's pleasure in writing about clathrate compounds.

SISTER MARY MARTINETTE HAGAN, B.V.M.

Chicago, Illinois
May 1, 1962

Contents

Contents

CHAPTER 1

Inclusion Compounds

An investigator confronted with the task of studying the vast array of known complex chemical compounds finds this task a formidable one. The confusion encountered results from the original use of the term "complex compounds" to designate all compounds in which the component atoms do not appear to obey the "normal" rules of combination. The number and varieties of these compounds appear to be without limit. Classification into such groups as molecular compounds, coordination compounds, inorganic polymers, and others represents a concerted effort on the part of chemists to bring order out of the disarray. However, there remain lines of distinction which are far from clearcut. Clathrate compounds constitute a relatively small segment of that group of complex molecules which has been designated as molecular compounds. An explanation of the general nature of molecular compounds is, consequently, a necessary concomitant to an introduction and development of a discussion of clathrates.

A new class of compounds in which bonding appeared to be different from that found in normal chemical reactions was first noted by Pfeiffer[196], who undertook to explain by the application of Werner's coordination theory[267] the existence of hitherto unexplained duo-crystalline forms of certain compounds and of compound combinations. Pfeiffer named these compounds, "molecular compounds," and further distinguished between those which were inorganic-organic and those which were organic. One of the early attempts to describe these molecular compounds was that of Hertel[122] who wrote, "A molecular compound is a substance formed from two different components each of which may have an independent crystal structure and which, in solution (or the vapor state), decomposes into its components according to the law of mass action. The force which holds them together in the molecular compound has been called secondary valence or residual affinity." Today this is neither a complete, nor a satisfactory description of molecular compounds, though it represents an attempt to provide some basis on which lines of demarcation between complex compounds may be drawn.

With the definition of molecular compounds as given by Hertel as a "working definition," Clapp[52] presented a classification of *organic* molecular compounds which further organized the field. He divided them into four groups:

(1) The products formed from benzoquinone, substituted quinone, or closely related compounds with aromatic hydrocarbons, amines, phenols, and aromatic ethers.

(2) The products of nitro compounds with aromatic hydrocarbons, halides, amines, and phenols.

(3) The compounds formed by the bile salts with fatty acids, esters, paraffins, and a few other compounds.

(4) The compounds containing a hydrogen bond.

Clapp also pointed out some properties which organic molecular compounds have in common such as: the ease with which many of them may be prepared, their tendency to decompose rather than melt, and their dissociation into their components when put into solution. Three possible theories were advanced to account for the structures of the molecules found in these four classes of organic molecular compounds, no one of which has been accepted *in toto*. Whether the structures result from the formation of a coordinate covalent bond between two components, a polarization of aggregates which negates the residual valences of the two parts, or from the formation of an essentially ionic bond caused by electron transfer from one component to the other remains undecided. The theory of the coordinate covalent bond breaks down in cases such as those in which an amine is replaced by an aromatic hydrocarbon, as is seen by comparison of the molecular compound formed from quinoline and *sym*-trinitrobenzene with that formed from toluene and *sym*-trinitrobenzene. In the compound formed from toluene and *sym*-trinitrobenzene, the donor and acceptor atoms are not recognizable. Possibly the theory s tenable if one pair of the pi electrons of a double bond in an aromatic hydrocarbon is considered to act as a donor pair—an assumption which appears to be widely accepted by organic chemists.

Polarization is readily recognized as a property which can bring about the formation of molecular compounds; however the polarization of aggregates caused by electrostatic attractions does not account for simple molecular ratios in the compounds formed. Molecules of marked size differences are not expected to react with molecules of a second component to give molecular compounds in which the ratios of the two components are the same, because the electron field about the components can not, of course, be uniform. However, surprisingly, the ratios observed between the two components are largely whole number ratios. While some investigators present evidence which would seem to justify the proposal of ionic character in the bonding of certain molecular compounds, x-ray analysis, in particular, contradicts the more tenuous evidence. Too, the strong crystal lattices which ionic bonds would produce are lacking as seen by the fact that the melting points of certain molecular compounds are lower than those of one, or both, components.

A group known as occlusion compounds, or inclusion compounds, is found in Clapp's third class of organic molecular compounds. This third class is composed of organic molecular compounds in which the chemical properties of the components are subordinate to the sizes and geometries of the molecules; the stereochemistry and size relationships of inclusion compounds play major roles in their behavior. Because the utility of the inclusion process has been only recently recognized, the unique characteristics of inclusion compounds have had limited application in industry and research. It is in this group of inclusion compounds that clathrates are found. Clathrates, in turn, possess novel structural characteristics which have yet to be completely exploited.

Though Clapp's classification is a workable one, there is no universally accepted classification of molecular compounds, nor does there appear to have been any attempt to arrive at one. When writing of molecular compounds, Ketelaar[139] refers to the van der Waals' forces which are actually one-tenth to one-twentieth as large as the energy of most atomic or ionic bonds; consequently they do not give rise to the formation of chemical compounds with stable molecules. Compounds in which there is bonding by van der Waals' forces include numerous "so-called molecular compounds." Ketelaar divides them as follows:

(1) Molecular compounds which have formed as a result of the favorable mutual orientation of their two components, each of which possesses a dipole, and include:
  (a) Clathrates.
  (b) Gas hydrates.
  (c) Urea adducts.
(2) Molecular compounds which are formed by the exchange of atoms and include:
  (a) Those in which the free electron pair of

the doner and the incomplete electron configuration of the acceptor are already present.

(b) Those in which they are not.

In still another account of molecular compounds, that of Robertson[237], attention is called to the fact that, though hydrogen bonding is perhaps the most universal and certainly the most studied form of molecular association, there does exist a unique group of molecular compounds in which hydrogen bonding plays a minor role, or is even nonexistent. Excluding all molecular compounds in which hydrogen bonding may be exclusively responsible for the bonding involved, four cases are cited:

(a) Molecular compounds formed between aromatic hydrocarbons and polynitro compounds.

(b) Addition compounds formed by polycyclic hydrocarbons with certain halogens or with antimony pentachloride.

(c) Loose addition complexes formed between unsaturated compounds and copper, silver, or mercury salts.

(d) Clathrates.

Compounds in which hydrogen bonding is negligible or absent are inclusion compounds and are so very numerous that they constitute a study in themselves. Schlenk[260, 264] first gave them the name "inclusion compounds," and, as indicated above, they are not infrequently called "occlusion compounds." Certain inclusion compounds, notably those of urea and thiourea, are commonly referred to as "adducts." Limiting this discussion to inclusion compounds, we find that they, too, may be classified into at least four main divisions. Baron[20] has listed these divisions as:

(1) Polymolecular inclusion compounds:
    (a) Those with channel-like spaces.
    (b) Those with cage-like spaces.
(2) Monomolecular inclusion compounds.
(3) Macromolecular inclusion compounds.
(4) Products of the blue iodine reaction.

Since this book is written for those whose primary interest is in one type of inclusion compound, the clathrates, descriptions of inclusion compounds and of the essential differences between the inclusion compounds as they are subdivided here, will be given, but only in sufficient detail to provide an understanding of the scope of the subject and the relationships between the divisions.

For the chemist who is a traditionalist, inclusion compounds are probably most clearly defined in a negative way. They are compounds which do not form by means of ionic, covalent, or coordinate covalent bonds. Inclusion compounds have been described as combinations of complete organic molecules that are united spatially, leaving unaffected the bonding systems of the components. Actually, inclusion is believed to be the result of the ability of one compound, because of its peculiar stereochemical properties and possibly its polarity, to enclose a second spatially. This second molecule may be of the same or different compound. The terms "guest" and "host" have been applied to the enclosed molecule and the enclosing molecular network, respectively. An essential characteristic of the host is its ability to form a solid structure with hollow spaces of large enough dimensions to house prospective

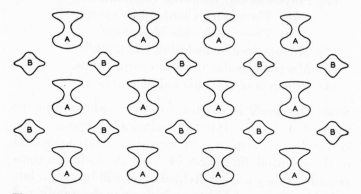

Figure 1-1. A schematic two-dimensional representation of a small region within an inclusion compound that is formed from molecules of a trapping component, A, and of a trapped component, B. [Copied with permission from G. W. Wheland, "Advanced Organic Chemistry," Chapter 4, p. 155, Wiley (1960)]

guests. The inclusion compound which forms will have a stability largely attributable to the way in which the molecules involved fit together in space. When inclusion occurs, the host and guest molecules must be properly oriented with respect to one another, under optimum conditions for formation. Wheland[309] illustrated this with a simplified two dimensional analog, Figure 1-1, using small irregular closed curves (B) to represent the guest molecules and similarly larger irregular closed curves (A) to represent the host structure.

The forces operating in the formation of inclusion compounds may be said, in general, to depend on the type of inclusion compound formed. Weak van der Waals' forces are considered very important, and highly oriented dipole interactions may be contributing factors. In certain cases, such as the ring-type structure of the cyclodextrins, a molecular arrangement with a center hollow space results. Normally, however, it is not easy to predict whether or not a compound will crystallize in such a form as to leave hollow spaces or, if so, whether these hollow spaces will be of proper dimensions to house smaller guest molecules. It has been established that the hollow space in which the guest molecule is enclosed may be a channel, a cage, or a layer.

As their name indicates, the polymolecular inclusion compounds are composed of polymolecular host structures. Those which have channel-like spaces include the very well-known urea and thiourea adducts or complexes. By x-ray analysis methods it has been shown that pure urea, on crystallization from a solvent, forms a loose hydrogen bonded tetragonal crystalline lattice. When unbranched hydrocarbon chain compounds are dissolved in the solvent, the crystallization product is an inclusion compound and has an hexagonal lattice. The hexagonal lattice is much firmer than the tetragonal lattice, indicating the value and importance of the guest molecule, the hydrocarbon, in the formation of a more compact structure.

Figure 1-2. Cross section of the urea-*n*-hydrocarbon complex. [A. E. Smith, *Acta Cryst.*, **5**, 224 (1952)]

Our knowledge of the urea adducts developed as the result of an accidental discovery by Bengen[31]. While conducting experiments with urea on pasteurized milk, Bengen found that, under certain conditions, the fat separated out in a manner which made it possible to determine the fat content of milk. Puzzled by what he thought was an emulsion, he added a trace of n-octyl alcohol to prevent emulsion formation; then he set the sample aside. Some days later he found urea-n-octanol crystals at the interface of the liquid layer. This incident prompted his investigations on higher alcohols, then paraffins; finally it led to a patented method for the separation of hydrocarbons[29].

Schlenk[260] and later Smith and others[270,271,301] studied the crystalline structure of the urea host and the urea-n-hydrocarbon complex by x-ray methods of analysis. Urea molecules were shown to undergo hydrogen bonding to form hollow channels large enough to accommodate the planar but angular (zig-zag) hydrocarbon molecules. Figure 1-2 illustrates schematically the packing arrangement as seen looking along the c-axis of the urea-n-hydrocarbon complex. The channel formed by van der Waals' radii of the atoms of the urea molecules is indicated. According to Smith, the hydrogen bonds between the hydrogen of the NH_2 groups and the oxygen of the adjacent urea molecules account largely for the stability of the complex. Figure 1-3 illustrates schematically the arrangement of hydrogen bonds. Although there is a slight tilt of the urea molecules to the plane of the channel wall and a displacement of the oxygen atoms from the wall intersections, for the sake of simplicity, these are not shown in the diagram. The covalent bonds are indicated by solid lines and the hydrogen bonds by dotted lines. There are three interpenetrating spirals of urea molecules hydrogen-bonded together forming

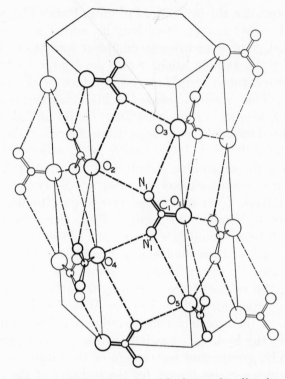

Figure 1-3. Arrangement of hydrogen bonding in
urea-n-hydrocarbon complexes. [A. E. Smith, *Acta
Cryst.*, **5**, 224 (1952)]

the walls of the hexagonal channel. Each oxygen is
hydrogen-bonded to four nitrogen atoms and each
nitrogen to two oxygen atoms. The hydrogen bonds,
which are essentially coplanar with the urea molecules,
are of two types. One is longer than the other. The
longer bonds, illustrated by N_1—O_3 and N_1'—O_5, are

about 3.04Å in length. The shorter bonds, indicated by N_1—O_2 and N_1'—O_4, are about 2.93Å in length.

Table 1-1 lists all the urea-n-hydrocarbon complex intermolecular contacts and the bond distances. While the stability of the complex arises mainly from the hydrogen bonding between the NH_2 group hydrogen atoms and the oxygen atoms of the adjacent urea molecules in the host, the van der Waals' forces between the hydrocarbon molecule, the guest, and the urea molecules which surround it contribute to the greater stability of the polymolecular inclusion compound. The van der Waals' contacts are less than normal in tetragonal urea; but in the hexagonal urea-hydrocarbon complex they appear to be about normal.

TABLE 1-1. INTERATOMIC DISTANCES[301]

Urea-hydrocarbon Complexes		Tetragonal Urea	
C—O	1.28Å	C—O	1.262Å
C—N	1.33	C—N	1.335
N_1—N_1'	2.30		
N_1—O_2	2.93	N—O	2.989
N_1—O_3	3.04	N—O	3.035

In Figure 1-4 the tetragonal urea structure with hydrogen bonding between adjacent molecules is illustrated and is shown to be a relatively open structure.

X-ray structure analysis shows clearly the existence of a central channel in the urea-n-hydrocarbon complex whose dimensions limit the size of the guest molecule. It is important, then, that the n-hydrocarbon be one in which the components have dimensions suitable to a guest whose position has been

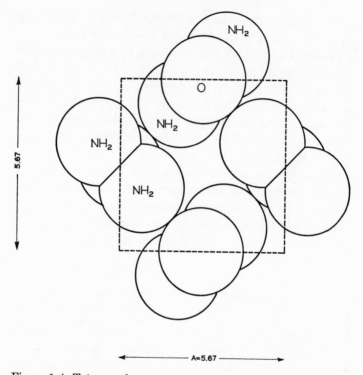

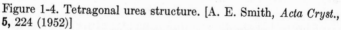

Figure 1-4. Tetragonal urea structure. [A. E. Smith, *Acta Cryst.*, **5,** 224 (1952)]

assigned in the channel. To illustrate this point, a hydrogen atom might be replaced in the *n*-hydrocarbon guest molecule by a fluorine atom which is of approximately the same size, but not by the larger bromine halogen atom. In Table 1-2 a compilation of useful information on some of the limitations of size of the urea guest molecules is given.

The thiourea complexes are, in general, similar to those of urea but they have channels approximately 7Å in diameter, as compared to those of urea which are approximately 5Å. Therefore, as would logically be expected, thiourea complexes will accommodate larger guest molecules such as trimethylpentane, cyclopentane, and triptane.

TABLE 1-2. UREA ADDUCTS[20]

Guest Compounds	Lowest Useful Member
Hydrocarbons	n-Hexane
Alcohols	Hexanol
Ketones	Acetone
Acids	Butyric
Halides	Octyle
Amines	Hexamethylenediamine

One of the largest compounds found to form a thiourea adduct is 2,6,9,13,16-pentamethylheptadecane which is approximately 22Å long. The shortest chain-length for the guest is limited energetically as well as spatially, but such energy considerations are not discussed in this book. The urea and thiourea hydrocarbon complexes resemble the clathrates in that the presence of the guest molecules induces the ureas to take configurations different from those of their normal structures. They differ from the clathrates in that both ureas form channel rather than cage structures.

The oldest of the recorded inclusion compounds are those of the choleic acids[310]. Desoxycholic acid and apocholic acid, which are formed by the addition of aliphatic acids to certain acids of the bile acid group, form inclusion compounds with a large number of compounds of varying types. These include some hydrocarbons and many esters, alcohols, carboxylic acids, phenols, ethers, and alkaloids. Certain facets of the chemistry of the choleic acids are challengingly unclear. X-ray studies on the crystalline structures of these complexes have shown them to have open structures[112,146]. Desoxycholic acid acts as an "enveloping shell" leaving a channel parallel to the longitudinal carbon axis for the guest molecules. Wheland[309] calls attention to the contradictory behavior of the crystalline complexes when in solution. However, studies on the crystal structures show the complexes to be inclusion compounds in which the choleic acids crystallize in open structures leaving free channels in the center. The more commonly known choleic acid complexes are those of desoxycholic acid. Particularly, the inclusion of carboxylic acids has been extensively probed. It has been shown that the number of C atoms in the aliphatic acid controls the composition of the inclusion compound. The effects are indicated in Table 1-3. Similar trends are observed with other series of analogous compounds. Choleic acids form channel structures which resemble, in some respects, the urea-hydrocarbon complexes. However, in the latter molecular complexes, the molal ratio of urea to hydrocarbon generally cannot be represented by integers or quotients of small integers.

These inclusion compounds of the choleic acids do not dissociate completely into their components in the liquid phase and therefore choleic acids do not exist, as such, in solution. The solubilization of the inclusion compounds quite likely should be attributed to a soap-like action of the salt of the acid. This particular characteristic of the complexes provides a method of solubilizing fatty acids, insoluble hydrocarbons and

TABLE 1-3

No. of C Atoms in the Acid Molecule	No. of Acid Molecules	No. of Desoxycholic Acid Molecules
1	0	0 (Formic acid does not form an inclusion compound)
2	1	1
3	1	3
4 to 8 (normal acids)	1	4
9 to 14	1	6
15	1	8

the like. The choleic acid group of polymolecular inclusion compounds has already been used in the separation of components of *racemic* mixtures[277]. Partial resolutions have been reported of such racemates as those of α-terpineol, camphor, sec-butylpicramide, and methylethylacetic acid.

The complexes which are formed between a large number of biphenyl derivatives and 4,4′-dinitrobiphenyl are another slightly different group. Robertson describes the host structure built up from the dinitrobiphenyl molecules as resulting from a "self-complex formation" governing both geometrically and sterically the nature of the acceptable second component, the guest. An idealized picture of the structure of these complexes is shown in Figure 1-5. The host molecules, shown by the heavy black dots, form a face-centered arrangement with three or four nearly planar molecules "stacked" on top of one another to form channels or tubes in which the host molecules are accommodated. There is no evidence of localized

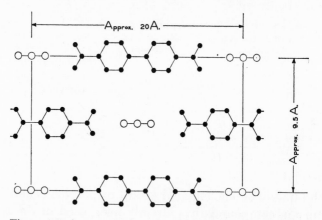

Figure 1-5. A cross section of an idealized structure of the dinitrobiphenyl adducts. [M. Baron, *Org. Chem. Bull.*, 29, No. 2, 4 (1957)]

bonding. As far as has been determined, the geometry of the structure governs also the molecular ratios of the two components. As a matter of fact, the molecular ratios for a number of the complexes can be calculated from a knowledge of the length of the guest molecules which will determine the corresponding numbers of the host molecules which will be required. The presence of numerous pi electrons should be expected to, and does, introduce strong electrostatic influences.

The list of common guest molecules in these adducts contains markedly nucleophilic molecules; among them are: benzidine, 4-bromobiphenyl, 4-hydroxybiphenyl, 4-aminobiphenyl, biphenyl, N,N,N',N'-tetramethylbenzidine, and 4,4'-dimethoxybiphenyl[20].

Channel-like inclusion compounds are illustrated by the foregoing types, that is, the complexes of urea, thiourea, the choleic acids, and dinitrobiphenyl. Baron[20] categorizes these as one of the two groups in the polymolecular inclusion compounds division of inclusion compounds. The other group is the cage-like inclusion compounds, the clathrates, which will not be discussed here, but rather, in the remaining chapters of the book.

A very interesting report by Barrer[23] on the spatial properties of some common types of inclusion compounds is summarized in Table 1-4. His study of the dimensions of lattices included the networks formed by hydrogen-bonded urea and thiourea inclusion compounds. Also included were the inorganic lattices of the crystalline zeolites—the most open of which is faujasite which easily occludes molecules of *iso*octane—and two different kinds of hydrogen-bonded water lattices. Barrer compared the geometries of the free volumes of the host lattices, contrasting them with the free volumes of the organic and inorganic lattices and defining his term "free," when used in relation to channel and cage dimensions as meaning "not occupied by the periphery of any of the atoms forming the continuous network." Accordingly, both water and hydroquinone clathrates have free volumes in the form

TABLE 1-4[23]. SPATIAL PROPERTIES OF SOME CAGE SYSTEMS

System	Free Diameter of Cage in Å	Free Diameter of Apertures Joining Cages	Free Volume Enclosed by Framework of Host Lattice in cm^3/cm^3
Hydroquinone-SO_2 clathrate	5.2	Small	0.09
Hydroquinone-Ar clathrate	4.2	Small	0.05
Urea-n-paraffin adducts	5.2	5.2	0.37
Thiourea-hydrocarbon adducts	6.1$_3$	6.1$_3$	0.41
Type 1 water clathrate, cage 1	5.2	Small	0.46
cage 2	5.9		
Type 2 water clathrate, cage 1	4.8	Small	0.46
cage 2	6.9	Small	
Chabazite	7.3	3.2 (4.9)	0.46
Zeolite 4A cage 1 ≅	7	≅ 3.2 _____	0.46
cage 2 ≅	11.8	≅ 4.9 _____	
Faujasite cage 1 ≅	7	≅ 3.2 _____	0.53
cage 2 ≅	12	≅ 9	
Gmelinite	≅ 7.3	≅ 3.2 (4.9)	0.46
Erionite	—	— —	0.44
Levynite	—	— 3.8	0.40
Harmotome	—	— —	0.35
Mordenite	—	— (4.0)	0.33
Analcite	—	— —	0.20

of separated cavities in which the apertures leading from one cavity to another have very small free diameters. The urea and thiourea inclusion compounds have free volumes in the form of continuous uniform capillaries, non-intersecting and all parallel to the hexagonal c-axis. The zeolites have a system of free volume cages which are joined by wide apertures to each of several other cages; consequently this results in a continuous system of intersecting channels with periodic varying free diameters along the lengths of the channels. Curiously, of all the host lattices compared here, the zeolites are the only ones stable in the absence of guest molecules and which permit migration of suitable small guest molecules from one cavity to another throughout the crystal.

Although polymolecular inclusion compounds constitute the majority of the recognized inclusion compounds, other interesting types are known. Monomolecular inclusion compounds are a second type and are so called because only one molecule is host to a guest molecule. Obviously the host molecule will be large and will have a cage-like space in its center. Typical of the monomolecular inclusion compounds are the cyclodextrins, occasionally called Schardinger dextrins because they were originally prepared by him in 1903[254]. These are produced by the enzymatic partial hydrolysis of starch, which yields molecules (a variable number, represented by n in the formula) of glucose residues joined together by α-glucoside linkages. The ends of the glucose residues are joined together by means of the same type of linkage to produce large glucose unit rings. A general structural formula of the resulting compounds is shown in Figure 1-6. Actually, three of these cyclodextrins, designated as α-, β-, and γ-dextrin, are known. Their formulas differ only in the values of n which are 4, 5, and 6, respectively. The internal diameters of the α-, β-, and γ-cy-

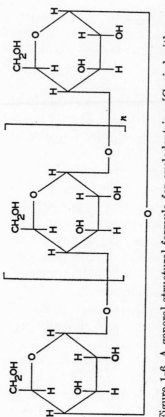

Figure 1-6. A general structural formula for cyclodextrins. [Copied with permission from G. W. Wheland, "Advanced Organic Chemistry," Chapter 4, p. 165, Wiley (1960)]

clodextrins are 6Å, 8Å, and 10Å, respectively. When in aqueous solution they rapidly form inclusion compounds upon the introduction of such molecules as trichloroethylene to α-dextrin, toluene to β-dextrin, and bromobenzene to γ-dextrin[100, 132, 309]. In each case the inclusion compound which forms is insoluble and immediately precipitates from the water solution. Advantage may be taken of this preferential behavior of the individual dextrins to separate them from one another by forming their respective insoluble inclusion compounds. If, after precipitation, the inclusion compounds are removed from the original solution, dried, and treated with boiling water, they decompose to release the trapped molecules and yield the cyclodextrin back again.

From the evidence available it would seem that both in solution and in the solid state the cyclodextrin complexes are inclusion compounds in which the guest components are held in the empty centers of the large carbohydrate rings, by van der Waals' forces[110]. The observed fact that the size of the trapped molecule increases from α-dextrin to γ-dextrin corresponds with the fact that the n values increase in the same direction.

Cramer has discussed briefly a number of other even larger structures which are similar to the cyclodextrins in their inclusion properties[59]. Stetter[289] characterizes the bis-N,N'-alkylenebenzidine compounds as very large molecules, each containing a ring which is capable, when crystallizing, of enclosing a molecule such as benzene or even of dioxane. Although some of these monomolecular inclusion compounds are only laboratory curiosities now, others have proved useful. Cramer used the cyclodextrins as host molecules in the partial resolution of racemic mixtures of mandelic acid ethyl esters as well as other esters and listed several minerals, graphite, cellulose, and some of the proteins also as monomolecular type inclusion compounds[65,68,69].

The third general type of inclusion compound is composed of macromolecules. Many articles have been written about these compounds[37,291], some of which have been described as "molecular sieves." The zeolites, among the best known, are macromolecular inclusion compounds whose inclusion properties have found wide industrial application. Essentially they are crystalline structures in which a framework of silicon-oxygen or aluminum-oxygen tetrahedra form the basic structure. They crystallize to provide a three-dimensional network which is permeated with relatively large channels and cavities. These interstices normally enclose water molecules which are removed quite easily, simply by heating the compound. The "holes" which are left by the evacuated water molecules can be filled with amazing numbers of gas, vapor, or dissolved compound molecules. An example of a naturally occurring zeolite is chabazite whose spatial characteristics are listed in Table 1-4. Both it, and anazite, are zeolites which, when activated, can enclose normal chain hydrocarbons. Barrer and co-workers[21,23,25,26,27] have made a thorough study of zeolitic inclusion compounds. A typical basic structure might be described as that resulting when two tight hexagons, each containing six silicon and six aluminum atoms and their associated oxygen atoms, face each other to form a fairly flat prism, and eight of these prisms link together to form a partially enclosed oval cavity which has a free diameter of 7.3Å. In turn, each resulting cavity connects with six adjacent cavities through apertures with a free diameter of 3.2Å.

Besides the naturally occurring zeolites, innumerable new types have been synthesized. It has been found feasible to synthesize them on an almost "tailor-made" basis, since control of the type to be produced has been so well worked out. Zeolites have been used to upgrade gasoline, to dry gases on a commercial scale, to separate hydrocarbon mixtures, as "carriers" for catalysts to prevent loss of valuable catalytic materials during the course of a reaction and, of course, commonly as ion exchange media[37]. As is well known, in this last connection, zeolites have been employed as water softeners for many years.

Lastly, the resemblance between the macromolecular inclusion compounds discussed and those of the lamellar intercalation compounds of graphite should be pointed out. In a sense the resemblance is marked, though the type of bonding may be quite different. The graphite stratified structure is one in which a guest may be accommodated between each stratum. Rudorff[238], Crofts[75], Hennig[121], and others have studied and reported the nature of these compounds. If intercalation compounds are included in the list of inclusion compounds, we may assume that inclusion may be in channels, in cages, or in layers. Even a cursory perusal of the literature will give convincing evidence of the fact that macromolecular inclusion compounds are an important and well-established group.

The products of the blue iodine reaction are set apart from all other inclusion compounds; nevertheless they are classified with them. Perhaps this is just one way of emphasizing their yet unsolved character. The blue color produced by the interaction of starch and iodine has been attributed by a number of investigators to a type of molecular inclusion and this seems to be well substantiated. Flavones, coumarin, benzophenone, benzamide, and barbituric acid are examples of other substances which give blue addition compounds[59]. Although much work has been done on these special blue addition compounds, their status is still somewhat obscure. Freundenberg[104,105,106] suggested that the iodine was located in the central channel of a screw-like starch molecule structure. However, later, from the analysis of the x-ray patterns of α-cyclodex-trin-I_2, benzonitrile-I_2, and coumarin-I_2 compounds, Cramer[60,61,64,65,67,68,70,73,74] observed that the iodine molecules within the compounds appear to be included not in the normal I_2 form but inside the channels in a polymeric blue modification. Even though Cramer has studied numerous blue iodine reaction products, his conclusion is that there still remains the question: why does iodine build up this chain structure only in inclusion compounds? The answer may lie in one of three plausible explanations: (1) a spatial "fitting in" of the I_2 chain; (2) polarization of the I—I bond, which causes "polymerization" of the iodine; or (3) interaction between the host and iodine in which the host may function as an electron donor. If the third explanation is accepted, the reaction may be written:

$$DONOR + I_2 \rightarrow (DONOR,I)^+ + I^-$$

In all blue iodine compound molecules such donors are present[59,173].

Schoch[266] reported the formation of an inclusion complex of iodine with fatty acids in which the starch chain appeared to coil around the fatty acids forming a host-guest structure, typical of *bona fide* inclusion. Even cellulose, in its swollen state, gives a blue iodine complex, which raises the question as to whether or not dyeing may be an inclusion process of some sort. In the numerous reports on the resolution of *racemic* mixtures by chromatographic methods it is tempting to speculate on the possibilities of inclusion as a key reaction. The ion exchange resins, starch, wool, casein, paper, and processed silica gel are all capable of inclusion of some kind.

In order to emphasize still further the fact that no classification of inclusion compounds has been universally accepted, it is pointed out here that Barrer[21] has preferred to divide inclusion compounds into three categories. He refers to the lattice of the frame-work forming component in the inclusion compound as the "host crystal;" subsequently he subdivides these host crystals into: (a) those which are stable without change whether included molecules are present or not; (b) those in which the content of the included molecules may be changed, but which, when this content falls below certain limits, become metastable to recrystallize completely; and (c) those which show a more or less continuous adjustment as the content of the included molecules falls or increases. Faujacite is an example of category (a). Urea and thiourea adducts and the hydroquinone clathrates fall into category (b). Montmorillonite intercalation complexes are examples of category (c).

In the case of each of the foregoing types of inclusion complex molecules, a literature search may wind deviously through a confusing maze of terminology. *Occlusion* and *inclusion* have been used synonymously. *Adduct* has frequently been substituted for *complex*. *Chemical Abstracts* uses the term clathrate as a generic designation encompassing all inclusion compounds. Layer type inclusion complexes, though usually referred to as *lamellar*, have been termed *intercalation* or montmorillonite complexes. The term *intercalation* has occasionally been replaced by *insertion* and has even been interchanged with *inclusion*. Powell astutely makes the observation that there is no precise line dividing certain types of inclusion compounds since what is a closed cavity for a large molecule may be part of a continuous channel for a smaller one[211].

At the present time, studies on the structures of the macromolecules of fibrous and globular proteins, synthetic fibers, cellulose, rubber, crystalline viruses, vitamins, and others are moving along at an extremely rapid pace. X-ray diffraction methods are of great importance in elucidating these structures. The inclusion properties of many of these compounds have been implied, yet, at this time it would seem premature to discuss any one of the types in detail. A great deal of fragmentary information has been collected but definitive structures are still lacking in most cases. Intramolecular folding as in the polypeptide chains, α-helix structures as in α-keratin, and the various forms of hemoglobin in whose wet crystals alternate layers of protein and liquid of crystallization are found, all indicate the eventual delineation of inclusion characteristics.

The gamut, then, of molecular compounds is long. The stretch known as inclusion compounds is not always clearly marked. To explore but one segment of the series is the work of this volume. As Powell has said, "The fit or misfit of molecular shapes is of fundamental importance in many chemical processes"[219]. We will now explore that "fit" of small molecules within larger ones which is called clathration. When, why and how it occurs, as well as the resulting products bear investigation; consequently new and profitable avenues of usage may present themselves.

CHAPTER 2

Structure of Clathrates

One of the first complete studies to appear in the literature on the structure of molecular compounds described the crystal structure of p-iodoaniline-s-trinitrobenzene[224]. This work seems to have been undertaken in order to settle a dispute regarding the nature of compounds formed between aromatic polynitro-compounds and other aromatic substances. The Fourier projections gave a picture which excluded the likelihood of covalent bonding between the molecules. Hydrogen bonding between the amino group and the oxygen atoms of the nitro groups was the only suggestion of any sort of chemical bond in the compound. An earlier proposal regarding the explanation of the formation of molecular compounds, made by Weiss[307], rested on the assumption of some partial ionic character within the molecule. A careful x-ray analysis was undertaken to evaluate this possibility since a study of the strengths of crystals will show if the component parts in the crystal of a molecular compound are held together by ionic bonds.

When the binding forces are only of van der Waals' type, the crystals will be of lesser strength than when electrostatic attractions between oppositely charged ions are also involved. One result of van der Waals' type bonding is seen in the fact that hardness and melting point values will be relatively low. Furthermore, decrease in intensity of all x-ray reflections as the Bragg angle, θ, increases will result because the thermal movements of the atoms are greater in the weaker crystals. A Weissenberg photograph shows a diffuse x-ray reflection spectrum of sufficient intensity that the effects of the weak interplanar forces may be observed. The diffuse character of the reflection may be interpreted as resulting from a large atomic movement perpendicular to a given plane. This is favored by weak bonding between layers[223]. Intermolecular compounds of such molecules as aniline with s-trinitrobenzene, p-chloroaniline with s-trinitrobenzene, and others, all gave evidence against the existence of ions in their structures. What interaction was present did not appear to be greater than the mutual interaction of like molecules within the crystals of the complexes.

In 1849 Wohler[314] described hydroquinone-sulfhydrate, a compound formed by the reaction of hydrogen sulfide with hydroquinone. Later it was observed by numerous other investigators that hydroquinone formed a series of molecular compounds with certain volatile molecules such as sulfur dioxide, hydrogen cyanide, hydrogen chloride, hydrogen bromide, methanol, and methyl cyanide. As previously mentioned, it was nearly a century ago that Mylius[175] concluded from his studies on hydroquinone with formic acid that, whatever the type of bonding in the compound which formed, it was not one of the then known types. He observed also that unusually large molecules form with hydroquinone and these compounds. To all appearances these larger molecules have an existence which is not explained by the union of components held together by any type of chemical bond. Mylius concluded that they resulted from the complete enclosure of the molecules of one compound by two or more molecules of a second compound and that, unless the strong forces which bound together the enclosing molecules were broken, the enclosed molecule could not escape.

Powell and his co-workers were the first to undertake a comprehensive study of the crystalline nature of hydroquinone complex molecular compounds, first carrying out a detailed determination of the structure of the hydroquinone-sulfur dioxide complex compound. By application of the very penetrating method of x-ray crystal structure analysis the positions of all atoms in the crystal array were accurately found. As a result of a tremendous amount of meticulous work on the Patterson-Fourier projections, an involved but exceedingly accurate picture of the molecular compound was produced. The hydroquinone molecules were shown to be linked through hydrogen bonds to form a giant molecule of three-dimensional proportions. They were of the expected size and shape and sufficiently separated from molecules of the other component to verify the assumption that there is no chemical bonding between them. A set of the hydroquinone molecules was shown to be linked together through hydrogen bonds between their hydroxyl groups. Six oxygen atoms of six different hydroquinone molecules form a plane hexagon. Alternate hydroquinone molecules incline upwards or downwards from the hexagon and are linked in a similar manner through their other hydroxyl groups to form a structure of the giant molecule type. Powell compared this structure to the steel frame of a large building in which each girder represents a hydroquinone molecule, and the points where six such girders meet form a hexagon to correspond with the hydrogen bonded hexagons. He showed that two identical hydroquinone frames of this kind form and interpenetrate. The result is a structure in which one hydroquinone framework is in no way chemically bonded to another hydroquinone framework; yet the two cannot break away from one another without breaking the chemical bonds of the interpenetrated giant molecule. Again, Powell compared this arrangement with two identical steel frames, not attached to one another at any point, but arranged in such a manner that the junctions of girders in one are at the centers of the rooms in the other[204]. This is illustrated schematically in Figure 2-1.

Powell showed that this double structure of interpenetrating hydroquinone molecules is not a very closely packed one. Between the two molecules is a set of cavities each of which is roughly spherical and about 4Å in diameter. Here may be found the guest molecule which, in the case of the hydroquinone-sulfur dioxide, is the sulfur dioxide molecule. All evidence, then, points to the association of two distinct components with one another to give a single-phased solid in which ordinary chemical union does not occur. The action which produces this complex compound is said

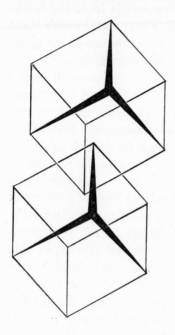

Figure 2-1. Schematic representation of interpenetration of two cage structures. (H. M. Powell, *J. Chem. Soc.*, **1948**, 66)

to be an imprisoning one and Powell observes that inclusion is favored by what he calls "the bad packing" of certain groups or molecules.

A more precise description of this large hydroquinone host structure is as follows:

"Six oxygen atoms form a plane hexagon of side 2.75Å parallel to the *xy* plane. The central lines of six quinol (hydroquinone) molecules extend alternately up and down from these oxygen atoms. The oxygen-oxygen axis of the molecule makes an angle of 45° with the plane of the oxygen hexagons, and, owing, to an inclination of about 3° to the line joining the corresponding origins, makes two slightly different angles of average value 111° *i.e.*, nearly the tetrahedral angle, with the hydrogen bonds at its ends. The angle between the plane of the benzene ring and the ZX_1 plane is 45°. Each of these six molecules is connected in a similar way through its other hydroxyl group to a separate oxygen hexagon parallel to but above or below the first[186]."

From this excellent crystal analysis, the picture of a true clathrate began to emerge. It was possible to postulate with regard to the nature of enclosed and enclosing molecules and to approach the study of other aspects of these compounds in a more formal and logical manner. For example, from this more precise description perspective drawings were made which are shown in Figure 2-2. Here the upper figure shows a continuation of the pattern of linkages in the hydroquinone framework which produces an indefinitely extending set of linked cages of general rhombohedral shape which result in a very open structure. From the lower figure it is clear that large central spaces or gaps form on each side of the cages and that a second identical framework structure can be inserted, being displaced vertically half-way between the top and the

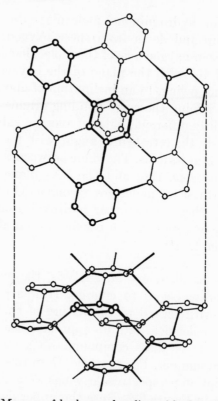

Figure 2-2. Manner of hydrogen bonding of hydroquinone molecules. Above: In plan each regular hexagon denotes six hydrogen bonds between oxygen atoms. Hexagons at different levels are represented by different line thicknesses. The tapered lines, representing the O—O axis of a hydroquinone molecule, show the method of linking to form an infinite three-dimensional cagework. Each taper points downward from the observer. Below: Perspective drawing corresponding to above. The hexagons denote the hydrogen bonds; the longer lines connecting different hexagons denote the O—O axis of the hydroquinone molecule. (D. E. Palin and H. M. Powell, *J. Chem. Soc.*, **1947**, 220.)

bottom oxygen hexagons. The atoms of the two inter-penetrating frameworks are found to be no closer to each other than those of similar normally unlinked atoms. Figure 2-3 illustrates the "cup" of three hydro-quinone molecules formed when they are hydrogen bonded. Although this is quite difficult to illustrate

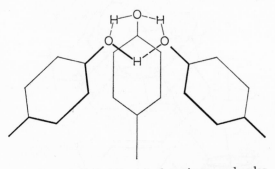

Figure 2-3. "Cup" of three hydroquinone molecules formed by hydrogen bonds. [F. Cramer, *Rev. Pure Appl. Chem.*, **5**, 150 (1955)]

by perspective drawings, it may be seen without dif-ficulty when shown stereoscopically. For further clari-fication, from Figure 2-4 it is evident that when the two frameworks have interpenetrated, there remain spaces in which small molecules will fit at normal non-bonded distances from the surrounding atoms of the intricate framework. These spaces are formed by oxy-gen hexagons of two different frameworks on what have been called the top and the bottom of the cavity and by the atoms of six benzene molecule rings on the sides.

Of prime importance in the determination of what kinds of molecules will be enclosed is their size. Structural relationships necessarily dictate this fact. Molecules small enough to escape through a given framework will not form inclusion compounds with it.

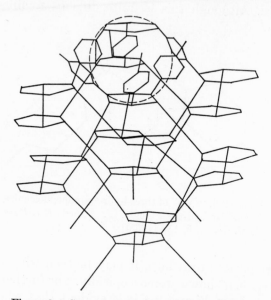

Figure 2-4. Structure of hydroquinone clathrate. The circle in the top shows one cage. [D. E. Palin and H. M. Powell, *Nature* 156, 335 (1945)]

Analysis of some clathrate compounds frequently indicates slightly less than the expected stoichiometrical relationships between host and guest molecules. This suggests that the total number of available holes may not be used. Why this should be the case is understandable in the light of the nature of the enclosing or imprisoning process. A guest molecule must be properly oriented at the moment of enclosure or it will not fit; hence it will be excluded. When this happens unfilled holes are to be expected.

The conditions which promote intermolecular compound formation are those which favor the formation of the matrix which is the host. The molecules concerned will tend to aggregate to give the most efficient utilization of space, rather than because of any mutual intermolecular attraction. This sort of behavior is shown by many familiar materials. Powell illustrates this point by calling attention to liquid metallic mercury, in its droplet formation, as an excellent example because here the atoms have on the average as many neighboring mercury atoms as possible[204]. Metallic crystalline structures in general favor close packing. It is commonly observed that molecules of different shapes tend to orient themselves in such a way that they fit together, like parts of a jig-saw puzzle. Large vacant spaces are seldom found—that is, there are no interatomic distances between adjacent molecules of dimensions either less than or greatly in excess of the van der Waals' radii sum. In crystallographic work this tendency to space filling is said to be brought about by the residual attractions which bring the molecules to a state of lowest potential energy when the packing is as close as possible[141].

This normal manner of crystal formation, however, may be upset in structures where several kinds of interatomic forces are in operation. When the forces are stronger than van der Waals' forces, as for example in water, the more open structure of the water aggregate is the result of the strong interaction through hydrogen bonding between one oxygen atom and its neighbors. In a similar manner the directed OH—O bonds in ice and the directed tetrahedral C—C covalent bonds in diamonds are responsible for open structures. In ionic crystals the contact of positively charged ions with those which are negatively charged may reduce other effects.

In each of these above mentioned illustrations the open structures are of relatively small dimensions. In order to obtain spaces of large dimensions, extended groups of linked atoms must be held by some type of strong attractive force to their neighbors. The zeolites, briefly discussed earlier, have been known for some time as molecular inclusion compounds which are capable of holding certain materials loosely within their polymeric structures[291]. However, as has been described, the spaces in the zeolites are normally channels, not enclosures, and one of the zeolite components may be removed or interchanged for another material of like size or charge.

In a similar manner linear metal-cyanide-metal rigid structures are found in certain complex cyanides, and their extended cage structures appear to be limitless. The cage bars have a M—CN—M length of 5Å or more, and their direction is determined by the metal[204]. Prussian blue is believed to have octahedral M bonds which result in cube-shaped cages. The complex, $KFeFe(CN)_6 \cdot H_2O$, forms cubic crystals in which iron atoms are found at the points of a simple cubic lattice, each iron atom is connected to its six neighboring iron atoms by CN groups which extend along the cube edges. The potassium ions and water molecules lie in the outlined cube-shaped cages. Similar structures were found when the M in $KMFe(CN)_6 \cdot H_2O$ was replaced by Mn^{II}, Co^{II}, or Ni^{II}[135].

When enclosure is desirable certain factors must be controlled in order that crystal formation may occur. Even though very open structures would result if a long linear sequence of atoms was used as the cage bar, or if the bonds were tetrahedrally spaced around the metal to form diamond-like structures, it does not follow that enclosure will occur. Clearly, under such conditions, it looks as if movement out of, as well as into, the enclosure will be unhampered. One concludes that the construction of cages having suitable spaces with holes small enough to prevent escape of the guest molecules may not be easy to effect by covalent bonds alone. Too, the presence of guest molecules in the right position for enclosure when cage formation is underway may not be favored.

To overcome these difficulties it has been suggested that atoms covalently linked to form groups of appropriate superficial extension be selected as the cage-forming components, and that each group be bound firmly to its neighbors at two or more points by some means other than covalent linkages. Intergroup cavities result in two illustrative cases. In the first case, schematically illustrated in Figure 2-5, the shape of the group necessitates this structure when packing occurs. The rigid portions of the molecules or complex ions which project make contact when crystallization occurs. The contact prevents more compact packing and leaves spaces which are able to contain another molecule at van der Waals' distances from its surroundings, even though these spaces cannot be utilized for better packing of the enclosing molecules. It is the

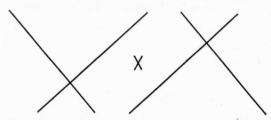

Figure 2-5. Schematic drawing: Two molecules of arbitrary shape are imagined restricted by their neighbors to movement to right and left only. They are shown at the minimum separations possible between their projecting ends. Space is left for another small component at X. (H. M. Powell, *J. Chem. Soc.*, **1948**, 62)

rigidity of the projections which prevents better packing of the host molecules. In the second case such effects as directional requirements of hydrogen bonds which link the host groups may complicate the packing procedure and lead to the formation of cage structures not unlike those caused by covalent links only.

One important advantage of the linking of a cage structure through covalence and some other form of binding, as in the first case mentioned above, is the fact that large exit holes may be blocked by the whole covalently linked molecule or other group of atoms if

either projects over the faces of the cage. The components of the host may be molecules or complex ions
capable of separate existences. Molecules of a desired
size and shape may be chosen, and the hydrogen-bond-
forming groups may determine their points of attachment, or, if the host is composed of complex ions, the
selection of appropriate oppositely charged ions may
be made. It is apparent that a thorough knowledge
of the structure and bonding characteristics of all components is required for anything even approaching an
accurate prediction of enclosure behavior.

Also, when enclosure is to occur, the molecule to be
enclosed must be in the correct place and oriented in
the right direction when the cage is closing. Should a
cavity form without enclosing a molecule the problem
of getting one in will be at least equal to that of getting one out. When the cage is closed solely by means
of covalent bonds, this difficulty is much greater then
when other conditions prevail. When the cage forms,
either in solution or on a crystal surface, by the ordered
arrangement of molecules or groups bound together
at numerous points, it is conceivable that there will
be a time before the space is completely sealed when
it may be penetrated either by solvent or by other
solute molecules. This is especially likely when the
solvent or other solute molecules are present in relatively large concentrations. Also, the cage may reopen.
If it does, and molecules or ions return to the solution,
it is highly probable that the large space on re-closing
will again trap a guest molecule.

An enclosed guest molecule may meet two obstacles

if it attempts to leave its enclosure. First, it may have to overcome an existing attraction between itself and its cage. Secondly, it may, and probably will, initiate an interesting series of reactions. When it approaches a possible exit point, or hole, its outward passage will be opposed by the repulsive forces that necessarily arise when any two atoms approach closely. As atoms approach one another closer than the equilibrium distances, the forces responsible for the relative constancy of effective atomic radii rise rapidly. If the cage molecules are held together by a strong mutual attraction, they will not be pushed apart readily, and if the exit holes are sufficiently small, the guest molecule seeking to escape will, on the contrary, be repelled inward.

The escape process may be considered as a type of dissociation reaction. When the enclosed molecule has transported itself to the middle of an exit hole from which it may pass with equal ease either into or out of the cage, it will have done an amount of work equal to its activation energy. The activation energy determines the rate of escape of the enclosed molecule. Such activation energies vary widely, differing with the structural character of the molecular cage, with that of the enclosed molecule, and even occasionally with different holes in the same cage. There is a high activation energy when the escaping molecules pass appreciably nearer than the normal van der Waals' distances to the cagework atoms or when the component parts of the cage may not be moved apart except by large forces because of their strong attachment to each other. The number of enclosed molecules having sufficient energy for escape is very small if the activation energy is several times the average energy for any given temperature, regardless of the distribution of energies among the enclosed molecules.

After the structure of the hydroquinone-sulfur dioxide inclusion compound was well-formulated and its behavior better understood, Powell made the observation that, "In the extreme case in which all escape is effectively prevented, except in conditions which destroy the cage structure, a new type of compound is distinguished[204]". With this statement clathrates were first recognized as a separate group of compounds. As Powell's research so clearly demonstrated, this new type of compound is a structural combination of two substances which results when the firmly bonded aggregate of enclosing molecules, the host, on crystallization entraps molecules of the other substance—that is, the guest.

Early in the study of clathrates a simplified and generalized picture of the nature of clathrate compound structures was proposed by Powell by the introduction of encirclement formulas. By using these formulas the basic concepts necessary for an understanding of clathrates may be more quickly grasped. However, when individual compounds are under investigation it is, of course, necessary to have recourse to far more complicated specific representations. The intricate crystalline structures of clathrate compounds are difficult to illustrate in two-dimensional drawings; nevertheless when encirclement formulas are used, a first step toward the understanding of their nature is taken.

To illustrate the use of the encirclement formulas let C represent the cage portion of a clathrate compound and let M represent the molecule which is enclosed. Using these notations the formula,

shows a simple clathrate cage and its guest component. The formula,

$$\left\{ \begin{matrix} C \\ M \end{matrix} \right\}_N$$

indicates an infinitely extended complex in a crystal. The subscript N outside the brackets is employed to show that the cages are infinitely extended and that there is multiple enclosure of each cagework by the other. The formula as applied to the hydroquinone-sulfur dioxide molecule, $3\ C_6H_4(OH)_2 \cdot SO_2$, may be written:

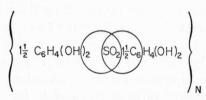

The interlocked rings denote mutual enclosure of two identical cageworks.

To explain the restrictions of the SO_2 molecule within the cage, Powell employed the diagram shown in Figure 2-6. According to this representation, the enclosed molecule, M, could escape by pushing apart the two independent portions of its cage against their van der Waals' attraction. This may require a large force, nevertheless if an attempt is made to enlarge the holes of exit, the cages will necessarily be brought together more closely elsewhere. Stronger repulsion

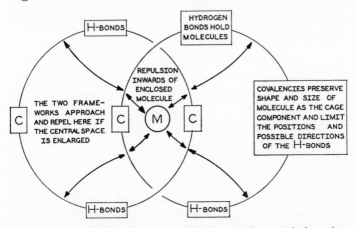

Figure 2-6. Diagrammatical explanation of the restrictions imposed by a host structure on a guest molecule in the hydroquinone clathrates. (H. M. Powell, *J. Chem. Soc.*, **1948,** 66)

forces will result and prevent enlargements of the exits. The effectiveness of these forces is contingent upon the stability of both the hydrogen bonds and the covalent linkages.

The general encirclement formula,

may be applied to all clathrate compounds. In this formula the combined symbol nM may be:

(1) A whole number, n, of molecules of component M.

(2) Any fractional amounts of two or more enclosed molecules that add up to a whole number.

(3) Fractional amounts, as in (2), with the qualification that one of the enclosed molecules must be present in some minimum proportions needed to trap the other enclosed components.

(4) Fractional amounts that do not add up to a whole number. This situation may arise when some of the cavities are unoccupied.

Following the first reports on the structure of the hydroquinone clathrates[55], Palin and Powell[186] undertook the structural examinations of other members of the hydroquinone series to determine whether a constant structural type was to be expected and, if not, to what extent the concentration and types of the enclosed molecule might vary the structure. The *beta* polymorphic form of hydroquinone which forms the interpenetrating framework with itself may be said, in so doing, to form a type of clathrate with itself. Hydroquinone may form stable needle-shaped hexagonal crystals of *alpha*-hydroquinone of density 1.35 g/cc, or the relatively unstable *beta*-modification which is characterized by being bounded by rhomohedral faces[46,47]. The density of the *beta*-hydroquinone is

1.26 g/cc. This empty *beta*-structure does not form readily when the solvent cannot be enclosed[129], thus indicating the stabilizing influence of enclosure or clathration.

The hydroquinone clathrate compound, in schematic diagram, appears large, loose, and flexible, moreover its ability to entrap other molecules apparently confirms the appearance. Molecules of widely different character are found to form hydroquinone clathrates provided they satisfy certain size requirements and do not react chemically with hydroquinone under the conditions necessary for clathrate formation. There is convincing evidence in clathrate compounds of freedom of movement of the enclosed molecules which, although they are firmly entrapped, are not necessarily closely bound to their surroundings.

The x-ray data obtained on a number of hydroquinone clathrates reveal conclusively that the cage structure has been modified in some instances and that the cavities need not all be occupied. The cell dimensions, and consequently the cage structures, vary slightly from one compound to another. The observed variations in the unit-cell dimensions are related to the dimensions of the enclosed molecule. The cage structure atoms are distributed over a spherical surface which is slightly less than 8Å in diameter. An effectively spherical molecule whose contact radius is at least 2Å could be entrapped without too close an approach to the hydroquinone atoms[187,188]. Molecules of hydrogen chloride, hydrogen bromide, and hydrogen sulfide meet this requirement. The other molecules listed in Tables 3-2, 3-3, and 3-4 are considered for packing purposes as roughly dumbbell-shaped. Palin and Powell use the configurations shown in Figure 2-7 to illustrate this point. In the diagram acetylene and methanol are represented by (I), sulfur dioxide and formic acid by (II), and carbon dioxide and methyl cyanide by (III). Because of the distribution of the

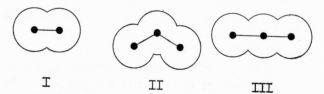

I   II   III

Figure 2-7. Schematic representations of molecular shapes: Acetylene (I), Sulfur Dioxide (II), and Carbon Dioxide (III). (H. M. Powell, *J. Chem. Soc.*, **1948,** 817)

surrounding atoms on the sphere with a relatively wide separation of the hydroxyl groups in their hydrogen-bonded hexagons at the top and the bottom of the cell, the axes of the dumb-bell shaped models must be placed vertically parallel to the c-axis of the crystal; otherwise proximity to the carbon atoms of the hydroquinone molecules will be too great. If the length of the molecules increases, the c dimension increases. The extensions of the cell along the c direction are conditioned by the lengths of the enclosed molecules. Acetylene produces no increase and methanol produces the smallest increase. Sulfur dioxide and formic acid give a large increase, as does carbon dioxide. Methyl cyanide gives the largest increase of those guest molecules considered here. Figures 2-8 and 2-9, respectively, illustrate schematically, a normal hydroquinone clathrate structure and a hydroquinone clathrate structure in which the cage has elongated.

Figure 2-8. Schematic representation of the enclosure of a molecule between two cage structures, e. g. hydroquinone. (D. E. Palin and H. M. Powell, *J. Chem. Soc.,* **1948,** 818)

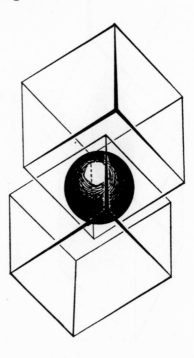

With an increase in the c dimension there is a corresponding decrease in the a dimension in nearly all observed cases. Powell assumes that in all of these clathrate structures the hydroquinone molecules remain linked through similar hydrogen-bonded hexagons of hydroxyl groups and that the hydroquinone

Figure 2-9. Schematic representation of the extension of a cage in one direction and contraction in the opposite direction caused by the enclosure of a "long" guest molecule. (D. E. Palin and H. M. Powell, *J. Chem. Soc.*, **1948,** 818)

complex host structure may be considered "hinged" at its points of attachment through its oxygen atoms. This he illustrates by the diagram shown in Figure 2-10. An increase in the *c* dimension and a decrease in the *a* dimension of the whole molecule is made possible by the hinge effect, which has been compared to a trellis in which angles may be varied without alteration of dimensions. Powell and Palin have discussed a number of individual clathrate structures at length, and the reader is referred to their work for a more complete picture of each separate compound[186–189].

Another clathrate structure exhaustively studied by Palin and Powell is that of the compound formed by

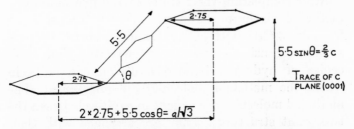

Figure 2-10. One hydroquinone molecule is shown with its oxygen-oxygen axis inclined at an angle θ to the 0001 plane. The two hexagons of hydrogen-bonded OH groups through which this molecule is linked to the rest of the structure are drawn in, and the way in which the angle θ may be related to either the a or the c dimension of the unit cell is indicated. The distances marked are in Å units. The hinging effect is obtained by variations in the angle θ. (H. M. Powell, *J. Chem. Soc.*, **1948**, 817)

hydroquinone and methanol. There was some confusion in the early investigations as to the nature of the product which formed when hydroquinone was crystallized from its methanol solution; however this problem resolved itself when the true nature of the crystalline product was determined. The allied natures of the structures of the sulfur dioxide and the methanol molecular compounds which form from hydroquinone is emphasized by the data found by means of x-ray crystal analysis. From the information obtained from the earlier study of the hydroquinone-SO_2 clathrate, some of the data for the hydroquinone-MeOH clathrate were deduced. When the electron density plot was obtained for the hydroquinone-MeOH clathrate, the similarity to the hydroquinone-SO_2 clathrate structure was verified[188].

After completing their study of the hydroquinone-methanol clathrate Palin and Powell assigned the formula, $3\ C_6H_4(OH)_2 \cdot CH_3OH$, and reported that its structure consists of two interpenetrating giant molecules of hydrogen bonded hydroquinone units in which the methanol molecules are imprisoned. The methanol molecules are caught in cavities between the two giant structures. They are arranged with their long axes parallel to the c direction of the hexagonal axes, and the structure is non-centrosymmetric. It seems probable that the methanol molecule is free to undergo considerable motion in the area around the axis.

One of the later studies on a series of this type of molecular compound is that made on the clathrates of tri-o-thymotide[156]. These clathrates are markedly dissimilar from those previously discussed. They have been divided into two groups, those in which a cavity is found and those in which a channel is formed. They are believed to have an enclosing structure in which van der Waals' forces alone are responsible for any binding present. The enclosed molecules are said to be relatively adaptable. The van der Waals' distances between atoms of the host and guest molecules vary by more than those for a given type of hydrogen bond. The cage-forming molecules have an arrangement which is influenced by their interaction with the enclosed component.

Tri-o-thymotide forms molecular compounds with substances such as alkanes, alkyl halides, alcohols, esters, ketones, ethers, etc. The typical clathrate compound which is formed has the general formula, $2 \ C_{33}H_{36}O_6 \cdot M$, and is found when the included molecule, M, has a length no greater than 9.5Å. When the molecules to be enclosed are longer than this, a channel-like structure will form; moreover the composition of the product will conform to the formula, $C_{33}H_{36}O_6 \cdot xM$, where x is a value which decreases as the chain length increases. Lawton and Powell[156] have published the x-ray crystal analyses of fifty molecular compounds of tri-o-thymotide. The cavity-type compounds include those of tri-o-thymotide with numerous groups of organic guest molecules, some of these are listed in Table 2-1.

Clathrate compounds of tri-o-thymotide are arranged in trigonal spirals, the two spirals passing through a unit cell ($a = 13.5$Å) and related to one another by a two-fold symmetry axis parallel to a. The "trellis" extension effect which was found in the hydroquinone clathrates does not seem to be present in these structures. Enlargement of the hole can occur in all directions. For example, the available space cannot be completely filled in the methanol compound which has nearly the same cell dimensions as the ethanol compound. As the size of the included molecule increases beyond that of ethanol, the cavity enlarges. Both a and c increase. There is no factor analogous to the hydrogen bonding of hydroquinone to link an increase in one direction with a decrease in the other. The enclosing molecules merely move farther apart. Evidently in the unexpanded structure there is a space

TABLE 2-1

Included Molecule (with unbranched chains)

ROH	where $R = CH_3$ to C_5H_{11}
RX	where $R = CH_3$ to C_4H_9
	and $X = Br$ or I
$X(CH_2)_nX$	where $n = 1$ to 3
	and $X = Br$ or I
ROR'	where $R = C_2H_5$
	and $R' = C_2H_5$

Included Molecule (with branched chains)

RR'CO	where $R = CH_3$ or C_2H_5
	and $R' = CH_3$ or C_2H_5
RCO_2R'	where $R = H$
	and $R' = n—C_3H_7$
CH_3CHRX	where $R = C_2H_5$
	and $X = Br$

nearly large enough to enclose the largest of the molecules which give the clathrate structure. Lengthening the chain of the enclosed molecule beyond a certain value merely results in the formation of the channel-type structure instead of the cavity-type structure.

The volume of the crystals for each tri-o-thymotide inclusion compound suggests the presence of approximately one-half as much space available for inclusion in the cavity-type structures as in the channel-type structures. Their selectivity leads to the conclusion that there are definite crosswise limitations within the cavity, and that probably the cavity is roughly cigar-shaped. This selectivity is illustrated by the fact that a small increase in the width of a molecule upon replacement of one substituent by another may prevent formation of the clathrate. The unit cell contains three included molecules which formally occupy either of the special positions $x05/6$ or $x01/3$, both of which require the molecule to have a twofold symmetry axis. A number of the included molecules have this symmetry, but many do not. For this reason some cannot be arranged in accordance with strict space-group symmetry; consequently the method of location of cavities by symmetry is limited. Lawton and Powell[156] discuss and interpret these observations.

Caglioti and his associates[43] have prepared still another and quite different series of clathrates. While complete structure information is not yet available, they have produced unmistakable evidence of the formation of clathrate compounds of cycloveratril. From the data now available, it appears that the formula for cycloveratril is that shown in Figure 2-11. Caglioti believes that the strong repulsions between the hydrogen atoms of the adjacent benzene rings, through rotations around the bonds between aliphatic and aromatic carbon atoms, may produce a stable *non-planar* configuration in which the benzene rings are tilted with respect to an average plane passing through the molecule. This non-planar shape would explain the formation of cycloveratril clathrates.

A molecule of this shape is expected to pack, in

crystal formation, in such a way as to leave open spaces into which smaller molecules will fit. While the structure is not yet clearly defined, it would appear that cyclic trimers are arranged in pairs in the crystal.

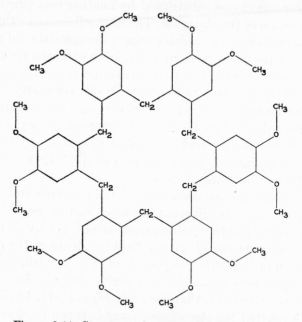

Figure 2-11. Structure of cycloveratril. [V. Caglioti, *et al.*, *J. Inorg. and Nuclear Chem.*, **8**, 572 (1958)]

Numerous clathrates of cycloveratril have been examined by both infrared studies, and, to a limited extent, by x-ray analysis. Some of the molecules enclathrated by cycloveratril are listed in Table 2-2.

The hydroquinone, tri-*o*-thymotide, and cycloveratril clathrate compound structures have been briefly discussed here in order to illustrate the extremes, *i.e.*, from the most detailed to one of the least detailed descriptions currently available in the literature. Powell and his co-workers apparently exhaustively studied the hydroquinone clathrate structures. Caglioti and his associates have initiated a study of the cyclo-veratril clathrates. As is normally the case in all such studies, only the limitations inherent in the methods

TABLE 2-2. SOME INCLUDED MOLECULES IN
CYCLOVERATRIL CLATHRATES

Benzene	Carbon disulfide
Chlorobenzene	Butyric acid
Toluene	Acetic acid
Chloroform	Thiophene
Acetone	"Decalin"

and instruments employed in analysis now limit the degree of elucidation. The specialists and those who are interested in any particular series of clathrate compounds are referred for such characteristically specific information to the original papers.

For more than a century the complexes of water with such simple molecules as those of chlorine have puzzled chemists. Davy[78] referred to the formation of some type of chlorine-water molecule and Faraday[91] proposed the formula $Cl_2 \cdot 10\ H_2O$. It was the work of von Stackelberg and his associates[278-287], of Claussen[54], of Pauling and Marsh[191], and of Nikitin[179,181,182] which clarified the nature of these compounds which had become commonly known as "gas hydrates." Among the substances which form these "hydrates" are: argon, neon, radon, chlorine, sulfur dioxide, methyl chloride, methane, and ethene. The picture which has finally emerged is one in which two crystalline clathrate forms are described. One form, Structure I, has a cubic cell constant of 12Å and forty-six molecules of water constitute the unit cell. Eight complete cavities are found in this unit cell, two of which are small and contain only one small guest molecule. The other six cavities can house relatively large molecules. The second form, Structure II, has a cubic cell constant of 17Å; one hundred and thirty-six water molecules are associated in each cell. These form sixteen small and eight relatively large cavities. For Structure II the following maximum composition formulas are possible[163]:

5.7 $H_2O\cdot M_1$, where M_1 is a molecule of the size of methane or hydrogen sulfide (12Å).

7.7 $H_2O\cdot M_2$, where M_2 is a molecule of the size of bromine, sulfur dioxide, or chlorine (12Å).

46 $H_2O\cdot 2M_1\cdot 6M_2$, the double hydrate (12Å).

17 $H_2O\cdot M_3$, where M_3 is a molecule of the size of propane, methyl iodide, or ethyl chloride (17Å).

17 $H_2O\cdot 2M_1\ M_3$, the double hydrate (17Å).

Recently Jeffrey and co-workers[7,133,168] have approached the subject of water clathrate compounds with renewed vigor. They have worked with over thirty crystalline hydrates and have reported that the structural unit is the $H_{40}O_{20}$ regular dodecahedron, Figure 2-12. It has twelve congruent regular pentagons as faces and is a noncrystallographic solid. Because of its fivefold axial symmetry it cannot be close-packed. Crystalline structures based on the dodeca-

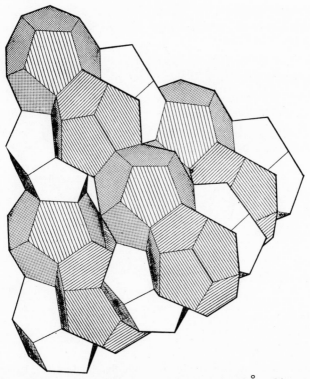

Figure 2-12. The polyhedral structure of the 17Å cubic gas hydrate cage, showing the pentagonal dodecahedra sharing faces "three-dimensionally." This structure has 136 water molecules in the unit cell. (Courtesy of G. A. Jeffrey, Crystallography Laboratory, University of Pittsburgh)

hedron are shown to contain nonregular "holes" which are polyhedra with hexagonal as well as pentagonal faces. These structural features favor clathrate formation.

The edges of the $H_{40}O_{20}$ pentagonal dodecahedron

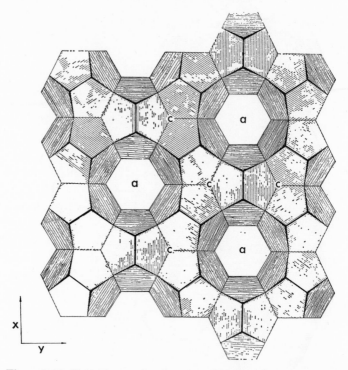

Figure 2-13. Tetra *iso* amyl ammonium fluoride hydrate. Layer of tetrakaidecahedra (a) and of pentakaidecahedra (c). (Courtesy of G. A. Jeffrey, Crystallography Laboratory, University of Pittsburgh)

are formed by thirty hydrogen bonds about 2.8Å long, which make a 169 cubic Å cage. Many geometric arrangements of the dodecahedra are possible. In the hydrates studied by Jeffrey the other polyhedra have twelve pentagonal faces and either two, three, or four hexagonal faces, making tetrakaidecahedra, pentakaidecahedra, or hexakaidecahedra, respectively, which have cages of volumes of about 216, 238, and 250 cubic Å each.

Of the crystalline compounds which have been studied by these investigators, five different types of crystal structures have been identified by single crystal x-ray diffraction methods. Detailed studies have been completed on $[(n—C_4H_9)_3S^+]F^-·20\ H_2O$ and $[(i—C_5H_{11})_4N^+]F^-·38\ H_2O$. The latter has the structural unit shown in Figure 2-13. The tri-n-butyl sulfonium compound has been shown to be structurally similar to the cubic chlorine gas hydrate. Jeffrey believes that hydration of this type could be significant in the complex systems encountered in biological processes.

The clathrate compounds which phenol forms with the molecules listed in Table 2-3 have been prepared

TABLE 2-3. GUEST COMPONENTS IN PHENOL CLATHRATES

Xenon	Hydrogen chloride
Hydrogen selenide	Hydrogen bromide
Sulfur dioxide	Hydrogen iodide
Carbon dioxide	Hydrogen sulfide
Carbonyl sulfide	Carbon disulfide
Methyl bromide	Methylene chloride
Fluoroethylene	1,1-Difluoroethane
Carbon disulfide + air	

and studied by von Stackelberg and his associates[280, 282] as well as by Nikitin and his associates[180]. Their structures have been described, and the maximum-composition formulas have been given[163]. These latter are:

12 $C_6H_5OH \cdot 5M_1$, where M_1 is a molecule of the size of hydrogen chloride or hydrogen bromide (four such molecules can be located in the large cavity.)

12 $C_6H_5OH \cdot 4M_2$, where M_2 is a molecule of the size of sulfur dioxide.

12 $C_6H_5OH \cdot 2M_3$, where M_3 is a molecule of the size of carbon disulfide (only two carbon disulfide molecules can be located in the large cavity and none in the small cavity.)

12 $C_6H_5OH \cdot 2M_3 \cdot M_1$, for the double clathrate.

The phenol clathrate compound is described as one in which each phenol molecule is associated with a planar hexagon composed of hydrogen bonded O—O linkages formed by the hydroxyl groups of six phenol molecules. The associated phenyl nuclei are alternately located above and below the hexagon. The six-membered groups are arranged in pairs with the hexagons opposite and parallel to one another. Between each pair a cage results in which one molecule may be imprisoned. The unit cell is rhombohedral with each corner occupied by the described arrangement of twelve phenol molecules. The rhombohedron, then, is an elongated cage which is three times the size of the other cages. There are twelve phenol molecules, one large cavity, and one small cavity per unit cell in a phenol clathrate.

One type of clathrate in particular has provoked intensive study. It varies from those first investigated in that the framework is inorganic. Powell and Rayner[225] prepared a group of clathrates by crystallizing them from an ammoniacal solution of nickel cyanide containing any one of a select group of organic molecules. They assigned them the general formula,

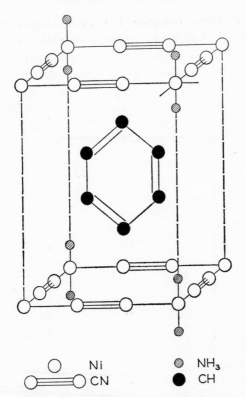

Ni

CN

NH₃

CH

Figure 2-14. Schematic representation of the clathrate compound, Ni(CN)₂NH₃·C₆H₆. (H. M. Powell and J. H. Rayner, *Nature*, **163**, 566 (1949)]

Ni(CN)₂NH₃·M, and the structure illustrated by the benzene clathrate shown in Figure 2-14, where M is benzene, thiophene, furan, pyrrole, aniline, or phenol. There is no obvious bonding between the nickel cyanide complex and the organic guest molecule. The crystalline benzene complex has been shown by x-ray methods of analysis to have an extended two-dimensional flat network as its main component. To each nickel atom there are two ammonia groups attached.

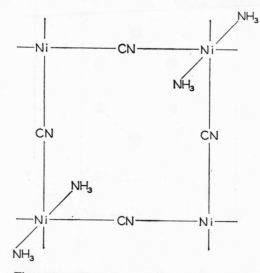

Figure 2-15. Simplified drawing to illustrate the rigid flat structure with projecting ammonia groups which characterizes the $Ni(CN)_2 \cdot NH_3$ cage. [H. M. Powell, "Weekly Evening Meeting," Roy. Soc. (London), April 27, 1951, p. 10]

These project above and below the network as shown in Figure 2-15. One set of nickel atoms is surrounded by four carbon atoms in a square pattern, whereas the other set of nickel atoms is surrounded by four nitrogen atoms of the CN groups and by two ammonia groups. The six nitrogen atoms form an octahedron.

Regardless of the arrangement of these structures, there will be empty spaces after packing has occurred. When the organic molecules, which fit conveniently into these spaces, are present for inclusion a well packed crystal will form[12]. Biphenyls form adducts with this nickel compound also. Leicester and Brad-

TABLE 2-4[245]. INORGANIC COMPLEX COMPOUNDS WHICH WILL FORM CLATHRATES WITH ORGANIC MOLECULES
(Arranged in the order of increasing number of carbon atoms in nitrogen bases*)

$Mn(4\text{-MePy})_4(SCN)_2$	$Ni(4\text{-Ac-Py})_4(SCN)_2$
$Mn(4\text{-EtPy})_4(SCN)_2$	$Ni(3\text{-NH}_2Py)_4(SCN)_2$
$Mn(4\text{-EtPy})_4(CNO)_2$	$Ni(4\text{-NH}_2Py)_4(SCN)_2$
$Mn(4\text{-EtPy})_4Cl_2$	$Ni(3\text{-BrPy})_4(SCN)_2$
$Mn(Isoq)_4(SCN)_2$	$Ni(3\text{-CyPy})_4(SCN)_2$
$Ni(Py)_4(SCN)_2$	$Ni(4\text{-CyPy})_4(SCN)_2$
$Ni(Py)_4Cl_2$	$Ni[4(Hyme)\text{-Py}]_4(SCN)_2$
$Ni(3\text{-MePy})_4(SCN)_2$	$Ni(Nicotinamide)_4(SCN)_2$
$Ni(4\text{-MePy})_2(SCN)_2$	$Ni(Me\ isonicotinate)_4(SCN)_2$
$Ni(4\text{-MePy})_4(SCN)_2$	$Ni(Et\ isonicotinate)_4(SCN)_2$
$Ni(4\text{-MePy})_4(N_3)_2$	$Ni(i\text{-nicotinic acid thioamide})_4(SCN)_2$
$Ni(4\text{-MePy})_4Cl_2$	$Ni(isonicotinamide)_4(SCN)_2$
$Ni(4\text{-MePy})_4(formate)_2$	$Ni(Isoq)_4(SCN)_2$
$Ni(4\text{-MePy})_4(NO_2)_2$	$Co(Py)_4(SCN)_2$
$Ni(4\text{-EtPy})_4(SCN)_2$	$Co(4\text{-MePy})_4(SCN)_2$
$Ni(4\text{-EtPy})_4(formate)_2$	$Co(4\text{-EtPy})_4(SCN)_2$
$Ni(4\text{-ViPy})_4(SCN)_2$	$Fe(4\text{-MePy})_4(SCN)_2$
$Ni(4\text{-}n\text{-PrPy})_4(SCN)_2$	$Fe(4\text{-EtPy})_4(SCN)_2$
$Ni(3\text{-Et-4-MePy})_4(SCN)_2$	$Cu(Py)_4(SCN)_2$
$Ni(4\text{-}n\text{-BuPy})_4(SCN)_2$	$Cu(4\text{-MePy})_4(SCN)_2$
$Ni(4\text{-BzPy})_4(SCN)_2$	$Zn(4\text{-MePy})_2Cl_2$

* (The following abbreviations have been used: Py, pyridine; Isoq isoquinoline; Me, methyl; Et, ethyl; Pr, propyl; Bu, butyl; Bz, benzy Ac, acetyl; NH₂, amino; Cy, cyano; Hyme, hydroxymethyl; Vi, vinyl; *i iso; n,* normal.)

ley[158] have shown that two rings may occupy adjacent cavities; however the structure is not yet determined.

Schaeffer, Dorsey, and others[245] observed the sharp selectivity of these inorganic host molecules toward organic guest molecules and subsequently prepared an impressive number of similar clathrating agents, some of which are listed in Table 2-4. The work on

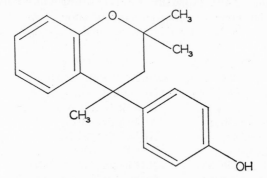

Figure 2-16. Structure of Dianin's compound. [W. Baker and J. F. W. McOmie, *Chem. and Ind. (London)*, **1955**, 256]

the uses of these compounds will be discussed in a later chapter.

Williams[312] prepared the clathrate compounds of cobalt(II), and nickel(II) tetra-(4-methylpyridine)-dithiocyanate with the dichlorobenzenes and with the methyl styrenes. *Para*-derivatives were shown to be enclathrated in preference to *ortho*-isomers.

Dianin's compound, Figure 2-16, has the empirical formula, $C_{18}H_{20}O_2$, and is a product of the condensation of phenol and mesityl oxide[17,81,82]. It has been known for some time to retain fixed amounts of certain solvents from which it can be crystallized. Powell and Wetters[227], as well as Baker and McOmie[17] investigated the crystals and concluded that Dianin's compound forms inclusion complexes with SO_2, iodine, argon, and innumerable organic molecules. There is strong evidence to support the view that these molecular inclusion compounds are clathrates. The compounds are very complex, and the structural details are not yet known but from an accumulation of evidence Powell and Wetters proposed the structure to be one in which there is one large cavity to six molecules of enclosing compounds. Using the encirclement formula, the formula for the clathrate may be written:

$$6 \ C_{18}H_{20}O_2$$
$$n\text{M}$$

where there are n molecules of M per cavity. A schematic drawing of this proposed structure is given in Figure 2-17.

The compound is described as having a form somewhat resembling an hourglass which has been cut horizontally across the middle of each globe. The waist forms the hexagon of hydrogen-bonded OH groups from which alternate molecules point up or down; three form the upper and three the lower cuplike structures. In the crystal, when these complex structures are piled directly on top of one another with their symmetry axes parallel to the c axis, cavities bounded

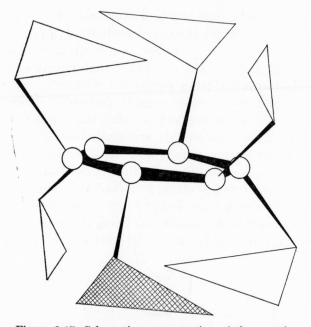

Figure 2-17. Schematic representation of the complex formed by Dianin's compound. One large cavity is seen in the center. Circles are OH groups. Lines pointing up or down from the hexagon of hydrogen-bonded OH groups are the links to the rest of the molecule which is denoted by a triangle. Shaded triangle is nearest to the observer from whom lines taper. [H. M. Powell and B. D. P. Wetters, *Chem. and Ind. (London)*, **1955,** 257]

by two neighboring groups remain. Strong van der Waals' forces between the one complex and its neighbor close the cavities. The number of molecules which can be fit into each cavity is, as usual, determined by their size. Mandelcorn[163] lists three maximum composition formulas for the fifty or more clathrates of Dianin's compound. These formulas are:

$6 C_{18}H_{20}O_2 \cdot 3M_1$, where M_1 is a molecule of the size of methanol.

$6 C_{18}H_{20}O_2 \cdot 2M_2$, where M_2 is a molecule of the size of carbon tetrachloride (two molecules per cavity).

$6 C_{18}H_{20}O_2 \cdot M_3$, where M_3 is a molecule of the size of ethylene dichloride (one molecule per cavity).

Table 2-5 lists some of the Dianin's compound clathrate guest molecules.

TABLE 2-5. RATIO OF DIANIN'S COMPOUND TO ENCLOSED MOLECULE[202]

2:1	Methanol
3:1	Acetic acid
	Carbon tetrachloride
	Methyl iodide
	CH_3NO_2
	SO_2
6:1	Bromobenzene
	1,3-Dibromopropane
	m-Dichlorobenzene
	o-Dichlorobenzene
	Ethylene dibromide
	Iodobenzene
	Tetrachloroethylene
	Argon

The unexpected results obtained by Hunter and his co-workers[130] in their attempts to purify the tetranuclear condensation product of p-cresol and formaldehyde from ethylene dichloride led to a proposal of clathrate formation. A stable crystalline 1:1 addition complex formed which was not decomposed even on heating to 90°C under high vacuum molecular distillation conditions. From ultraviolet absorption spectra data taken on a solution of the addition complex the investigators were forced to the conclusion that no form of enhanced dipole association had occurred. A molecular model based on the accepted van der Waals' radii showed that an ethylene dichloride molecule could be inserted under the more compact configuration of the polymer. This fact explains the case with which crystallization occurs in the form of the clathrate, as contrasted with the difficulty experienced with other solvents.

One clathrate compound of the formula, Fe-$(CNCH_3)_6Cl_2\cdot 3\ H_2O$, has been prepared[221]. X-ray methods of analysis show that the unit cell is formed by packing two hexagonal layers of Fe(II) ions with the CH_3CN groups projecting octahedrally from each iron. Four adjacent empty spaces result. The two chloride ions are so located that two dissimilar closed cavities result. Two water molecules are contained in one of them, whereas the third water molecule is in the other.

Saunder[230,231,241] and others carried out an extensive x-ray analysis on the molecular compounds of 4,4'-dinitrodiphenyl with 4-hydroxydiphenyl in which they showed all of the molecules to be approximately equally spaced from one another. This was one of the early reports on a type of molecular complex formation which depends directly on the crystalline state of the compound and which does not require the more or less complex interactions described for many molecular compounds. None of the intermolecular distances were shorter than those which are normally found in crystals of aromatic nitro compounds where the bonding is attributed to ordinary Van der Waals' forces. Among the molecular compounds of this group which they studied there was only one in which an exception was noted. In that one case an OH-O distance of 3Å was measured. Consequently, in that particular compound, the investigators felt that bonding "might be possible." Their conclusion with regard to the series of 4,4'-dinitrodiphenyl molecular compounds was that the requirements of crystal structure, rather than any bonding mechanism, were responsible for the observed stoichiometric ratios.

The work of Milgrom[170] on the inclusion complexes of methyl naphthalenes indicated the possibility of their clathrate formation with both straight- and branched-chain hydrocarbons, and with one type to the exclusion of the other. Although the type of inclusion is not described, it is of interest that Arcos and Arcos[9] describe disulfide bridges between protein layers. The bridges set the spaces between layers available for some type of penetration by carcinogenic hydrocarbons at roughly 6Å.

Lastly, the question of whether or not the α-cyclodextrin-gas complexes are clathrates appears unresolved. Cramer and Henglein[72] have reported some evidence in favor of their clathrate nature. Unquestionably there are many more clathrate compounds which are yet to be identified and/or prepared, and those which have been mentioned here will serve to demonstrate their universality.

The structures described thus far satisfy the description first given for clathrate compounds by Powell:

"A possible type of intermolecular compound formation involves the complete enclosure of a molecule by one or more molecules of another component in such a way that it cannot escape from its position unless strong forces holding its surroundings together are overcome. The enclosed molecule must then remain in association with its surroundings as firmly and as permanently as the parts of these surroundings are held to each other. This provides a means of uniting together different substances which may have very little attractive interaction. The form of enclosure required for such a compound is that of finite atomic groups or infinitely extended complexes that contain spaces of size great enough to hold a molecule of the second component. The spaces must also be bounded in such a way that escape of the enclosed molecule is prevented[204]."

Whether or not this description will give way to a more flexible and inclusive one remains to be seen. There is some indication now that it may do so, and that clathrates and inclusion compounds have a disappearing line of demarcation; furthermore what may be a series of cavities to one molecule may, at the same time, be a channel to another smaller molecule. At the present time completeness of imprisonment—in the exact sense of the word—would seem to be the hallmark of a true clathrate.

CHAPTER 3

Properties of Clathrates

Clathrate compounds exhibit the general behavior characteristics of molecular compounds. Because of their complex nature they will have some properties which are distinctly those of the host component, others which indicate the presence of the guest component, and variations resulting from the mutual effects of the two in such close proximity.

At best, all molecular compounds vary greatly in their inherent stabilities, as in all of their properties. When heated, organic molecular compounds tend to decompose rather than to melt[52]. It is commonly observed that some molecular compounds exist only in a solid crystalline lattice form. The examination of crystals by x-ray methods has, in a sense, abolished the molecule for some compounds. After the atom or ion the next larger distinguishable entity in the structure is not the supposed molecule, containing atoms in the correct ratio to explain the composition, but the crystal as a whole or some other indefinitely extended complex[202]. Often the crystalline molecular compounds will decompose into their components when put into solution or when subjected to some mechanical method of separation, for example, grinding. Some can be recrystallized from solution since they retain their identities as ions or molecules when dissolved[171].

The influence of the solvent is quite important. If either component is insoluble in a given solvent, the molecular compound will always decompose, which is indicative of the characteristically weak bonding in molecular compounds. Inter-atomic distances have been used as criteria of crystal strength; however, as discussed in the previous chapter, Powell and Huse carried out a study in which they showed that *without* inter-atomic distance data crystal strengths may be estimated and used to decide whether the component parts of a molecular compound are held together by ionic bonds.

It is observed generally that when the electrostatic attraction between oppositely charged ions is one of the binding forces in a crystal, the crystal will have greater strength than one containing molecules of comparable shape but held by weaker forces such as van der Waals'. Greater hardness and higher melting points also accompany the ionic bonding. Weakly bonded molecular compound crystals will display greater thermal movements of the atoms. As pointed out, this change in thermal movement will be evidenced in a declining in the intensity of the x-ray reflections as the Bragg angle, θ, increases. The interpretations of Powell and Huse[223] may then be applied.

Table 3-1 provides the melting point data for several typical molecular compounds and the melting points of their components. A molecular compound usually melts at a lower temperature than that of one of its components. When the two components have nearly the same melting point, the molecular compound may melt at a temperature lower than that of either component.

TABLE 3-1. MELTING POINTS OF COMPONENTS A AND B AND THEIR MOLECULAR COMPOUND AB[223]

		Melting Points, °C		
A	B	A	B	AB
Aniline	s-Trinitrobenzene	−8°	122°	123°
2,4,6-Tribromoaniline	s-Trinitrobenzene	118.5	122	108.5
p-Chloroaniline	s-Trinitrobenzene	71	122	110
p-Iodoaniline	s-Trinitrobenzene	63	122	108
3,5-Diiodo-p-toluidine	s-Trinitrobenzene	125.5	122	95.5
Hexamethylbenzene	Picryl chloride	164	83	148
Hexamethylbenzene	Picryl bromide	164	122	151
Hexamethylbenzene	Picryl iodide	164	165	145

Orchin[185] drew up four generalizations regarding molecular complex formation. Based mainly on his observations on picric acid, they are:

(1) Picrate formation (with hydrocarbons) results from the interaction of acceptor centers on one or more nitro groups with one or more donor centers.

(2) The melting point of the complex can generally be used to estimate its stability.

(3) The donor centers of the hydrocarbons must be suitably spaced for effective complexing with the nitrogen acceptor centers.

(4) If the hydrocarbon is non-planar complex formation is decreased.

Later a study of the series of complexes of 2,4,7-trinitrofluorenone (TNF) and the monomethyl derivatives of 1,2-benzanthracene and benzo(c)phenanthrene[290] revealed Orchin's second generalization to be invalid and further demonstrated the validity of the fourth one. Newman[176] proposed a fifth generalization, namely:

(5) If at least one nitro group is prevented from assuming a co-planar arrangement with the attached ring, the polynitro compound will be a less effective complexing agent.

Mullikin[173] developed a simple quantum mechanical theory to explain the interaction of electron acceptors and donors (Lewis acids and bases) to form $1:1$ or $n:1$ molecular compounds which range from loose complexes to stable compounds. The theory involves resonance between no-bond structures (A,B) and dative structures (A^-,B^+), where A is an acceptor atom, molecule, or ion and B is a donor atom, molecule, or ion. In a later paper[174] he commented that while the theory provided a correct general account of major aspects of the structure of molecular complexes, its application to detailed structures of particular types of complexes presents a variety of problems.

Robertson[237], in his discussion of certain aromatic molecular compounds, observes that there is, at times, no question of the formation of any exceptional or stable covalent bond between the components. Following Mulliken, however, he notes that in some cases there may be a mechanism of the general type in which an attraction of a Lewis acid-base nature is observed. For example, in p-nitroaniline bonding may be between the donating electrons of the benzene ring and the accepting orbitals of the nitro group. Of course the strength of the interaction will vary, depending on the aromatic substituents present. The variations will range from complete electron transfer to slight overlap of the orbitals, with resonance between the no-bond structure and the charge transfer, or ionic structure.

In summarizing the views of the majority of investigators who have been working with molecular addition compounds, AB, two all inclusive factors have been proposed by Ferguson[92] to account for molecular compound stabilities. These are: (1) the amount of polarization which occurs between components A and B which will be a major consideration, or (2) the steric requirements of A and/or B which will be influential.

The host components of clathrate compounds are composed of molecules which have those molecular properties which lead to the formation of open structures. Close packing in the crystalline state usually is indicative of relatively symmetrical molecules and of a strong molecular dipole. With close packing the intermolecular distances are small so that in the crystal lattice it is unlikely that empty spaces of any notable size will form. The situation is reversed in the case of molecules which are angular in shape and have permanent molecular dipoles. They readily undergo orientations and intermolecular interactions when crystallizing. Open molecular arrangements result, which are essential for a clathrate structure. One important characteristic of structures in which the cavities are closed is that there must be a fixed ratio of cavities to surrounding molecules.

The hydroquinone molecule and its molecular compounds whose structures have been discussed at length in Chapter 2 illustrate this well. The general series of molecular compounds which hydroquinone forms with the inert gases has the formula $3\ C_6H_4(OH)_2 \cdot M$, where M is the atom of inert gas. These compounds must be prepared under high pressure conditions because of the normally low solubility of the gases to be enclathrated. The pressure is not required to prevent dissociation because once the gas atom is entrapped it will be retained by the strength of its cage. The solubilities in water of the inert gases increase with increasing atomic number. Since the higher the solubility the greater the chance of an inert gas atom being available in the right place for enclosure, it may be predicted that that hydroquinone-inert gas clathrate will form most readily which contains the inert gas atom of highest atomic number.

There is a tendency in each case for less than the stoichiometrical amount of inert gas to become entrapped, presumably because the crystal structure builds up faster than the gas atoms can attain positions favorable for enclosure. A product of the enclathration of argon in hydroquinone in which the argon content has the maximum value found in the literature has the composition, $3\ C_6H_4(OH)_2 \cdot 0.8\ Ar$. The clathrate is "short" 0.2 gram-atoms of argon per mole of clathrate compound.

It has been calculated that the volume of one mole of the crystalline substance having the formula, $3 C_6H_4(OH)_2 \cdot Ar$, will be approximately 260 cc. If the gram-atom of argon present in this crystalline material were to occupy the same volume, that is 260 cc, when free of its hydroquinone cage at 15°C it would have to be kept under a pressure of 91 atmospheres! This amazing fact immediately suggests possible uses for clathration as a means of inert gas storage.

Efforts to prepare hydroquinone-helium clathrates have not been successful, probably because the helium atoms are small enough to escape from the hydroquinone cage structure. From his work on numerous hydroquinone clathrates Powell concludes that spherical atoms 2Å in diameter, or somewhat larger, will be enclosed and retained by the hydroquinone cage. From crystal structure examinations the radii of the inert gas atoms for temperatures at which these substances solidify are: Ne = 1.61Å, Ar = 1.9Å, Kr = 2.0Å, Xe = 2.2Å. The radii obtained from the interatomic distance field at room temperature will be somewhat greater because of increased lattice vibrations.

Many hydroquinone clathrates of other than inert gas molecules have been prepared also. As early as 1910 molecular compounds of hydroquinone-hydrogen halides were reported in the literature[114,265]. Table 3-2 offers some of the results of the structural examination of a number of them, and all of the compounds listed

TABLE 3-2[188]

M	Morphology, Forms in Rhombohedral Indices	Refractive Indices, n_D: ω	ϵ	Double Refrn.	Axial Ratio: From Interfacial Angle	2c/a from X-ray Examntn.
SO_2	Yellow hexagonal prisms (101) with (100)	1.62_9	1.65_5	$+0.02_6$	0.714	0.714
SO_2 (specimen B)	As above but poorly formed	—	—	—	—	0.680
MeOH	Colorless prisms ($10\bar{1}$) with (100 and $11\bar{1}$)	1.63_0	1.62_4	-0.00_6	0.66_4	0.67_1
MeCN	Colorless prisms ($10\bar{1}$) with (100), (110), and (211)	1.60_6	1.66_6	$+0.06_0$	0.78_3	0.78_0
$H \cdot CO_2H$	Colorless prisms ($10\bar{1}$) with (100) and ($21\bar{1}$)	1.61_3	1.63_3	$+0.02_0$	0.68_8	0.68_9
CO_2	Colorless	—	—	—	—	0.72_0
HCl	Colorless	1.63_2	1.62_3	-0.00_9	—	0.66_0
HBr	Brown	—	—	—	—	0.66_2
H_2S	Colorless	1.65_1	1.63_5	-0.01_6	—	0.66_3
C_2H_2	Colorless	1.63_2	1.61_2	-0.02_0	—	0.65_7
SO_2 + MeOH	Similar to SO_2 above	—	—	—	—	0.70_1
SO_2 + HCl	Pale yellow hexagonal prisms	1.63_0	1.62_9	-0.00_1	—	0.67_3

82

were obtained in a stable crystalline form. Tables 3-3 and 3-4 give the data found from the x-ray diffraction patterns and chemical analyses which were worked out. Q represents the hydroquinone molecule and M represents the enclosed molecule. The similarities between different hydroquinone clathrate compounds is determined by the data tabulated.

The guest component of a clathrate compound exerts a vital influence in certain instances, for example, when it directly affects the type of crystalline structure or when it notably controls the tendency to crystallization. Hydroquinone crystallizes from most common solvents in what is known as its α-form. When it enclathrates the solvent as in the case of methanol or when it enclathrates some other solute, it forms the β-hydroquinone structure. Similarly, monammine-nickel(II) cyanide is not readily crystallized because of the restrictive effect of the projecting ammonia groups on the layers of the complex. The ammonia groups cause the formation of large vacancies which do not favor crystal formation. The addition of a compound like benzene, whose molecules fit well into the vacancies, effects relatively rapid crystallization.

While the host structure of the clathrate compound determines the size and shape of the guest which it will enclose, there may be certain weak interactions between a guest molecule and its cage. They range from weak van der Waals' intermolecular attractions to definitely oriented dipole contacts. The stability of the complex is dependent upon these forces; however the combination of host and guest is transferred from

TABLE 3-3[188]

Added Molecule M	Mol. Wt. of M	Cell Dimension, kX U a	Cell Dimension, kX U c	d*	Ideal Formula 3 Q.M. Formula Wt. for 3(3QM)	Ideal Formula 3 Q.M. M %	From X-ray Results: Mol. Wt. per Unit Cell, Obs.	From X-ray Results: M %	From X-ray Results: Mol. Ratio M/3Q	From Chemical Analysis: M %	From Chemical Analysis: Mol. Ratio M/3Q
HCl	36.5	16.55	5.46	1.38	1100	9.97	1083	8.6	0.85	8.58	0.85
HBr	81	16.57	5.48	1.36	1233	19.7	1075	7.9	0.35	8.1	0.36
H$_2$S	34	16.58	5.49	1.34	1194	9.35	1060	6.5_5	0.69	6.2	0.64
C$_2$H$_2$	26	16.63	5.46	1.31	1068	7.31	1038	4.6	0.62	—	—
MeOH	32	16.56	5.55	1.35	1086	8.85	1078	8.1	0.92	8.6	0.97
H·CO$_2$H	46	16.42	5.65	1.37	1128	12.23	1096	9.7	0.79	10.2	0.82
SO$_2$	64	16.29	5.81	1.44	1182	16.25	1165	14.8	0.91	14.5	0.88
CO$_2$	44	16.17	5.82	1.36	1122	11.77	1087	8.9	0.74	8.9	0.74
MeCN	41	15.95	6.24	1.33	1113	11.06	1108	10.7	0.96	11.0	0.99
SO$_2$(b)	—	16.49	5.60	1.32	1182	16.25	1056	6.2	0.34	ca. 5†	—
SO$_2$ + MeOH	—	16.35	5.73	1.40	—	—	1125	—	—	—	—
SO$_2$ + HCl	—	16.47	5.54	1.39_5	—	—	1100	—	—	3.86	0.22
										5.78	0.58

Q = hydroquinone
*d = density.
† Sample not homogeneous.

Table 3-4[188]

M	θ, Calc. from a	θ, Calc. from c	M	θ, Calc. from a	θ, Calc. from c	M	θ, Calc. from a	θ, Calc. from a
HCl HBr } * H₂S	42° 10′	41° 40′	MeOH	42° 21′	42° 18′	MeCN	47° 36′	49° 10′
			H·CO₂H	43 37	43 14	SO₂(B)	43 2	42 46
			SO₂	44 36	44 41	SO₂ + MeOH	44 5	44 2
C₂H₂	41 42	41 28	CO₂	45 46	44 55	SO₂ + HCl	43 12	42 13

* For these three very similar unit cells the average dimensions a = 16.57, c = 5.48 were used.

a clathrate compound to a new molecular species if these forces are of any degree of magnitude. This distinction is illustrated when a comparison is made between a solution of hydrogen sulfide in water, from which a clathrate compound can be crystallized, and a solution of hydrogen chloride in water which will not yield a clathrate, but will form hydronium and chloride ions.

The properties of the clathrate compounds of tri-o-thymotide illustrate the influence exerted by the size of the guest molecules. The channel, rather than the cage, inclusion compound will form if the molecules to be enclosed are too long, similarly the guest molecules must also not be too small. One of the readily enclosable molecules is methyl bromide which is a gas at room temperature, and its tri-o-thymotide clathrate decomposes readily. Other tri-o-thymotide clathrates may be heated to 100° above the normal boiling point of the guest molecule without loss of weight. The smaller the guest molecules, for example Ar or CO_2, the less probable will be their enclathration. Tables 3-5 and 3-6 list data on the properties of many adducts of tri-o-thymotide with unbranched and branched molecules.

In Chapter 2, a number of hydrates were described as clathrates. They have been shown by x-ray studies to be compounds in which the "hydrated" molecules are entrapped by a lattice of water molecules. The thermodynamic data and lattice constants for some of them are given in Table 3-7. The clathrates listed in the upper part of the table are believed to crystallize to give Structure I. Structure II is much more complex[54,285], and the hydrates tabulated in the lower part of the table are believed to have Structure II. Also, the mixed hydrates probably have Structure II, in which case the larger molecules such as CH_3I will be found in the larger cavities, whereas smaller molecules like CO_2 will be present in the smaller cavities[284].

The monamminenickel(II) cyanide and analogous clathrate compounds are very numerous. That of the enclathrated benzene molecule in the monammine-nickel(II) cyanide crystals is one which has been most thoroughly studied[232,233]. The benzene molecule in the compound has been shown to be firmly held. At room temperature there is no detectable benzene pressure.

TABLE 3-5. ADDUCTS OF TRI-o-THYMOTIDE WITH UNBRANCHED MOLECULES[156]

Included Molecule (A) R·OH, Where R =	Calc. Length of Included Molecule in Extended Form in (Å)	Structure Types
CH_3	4.6	Cavity
C_2H_5	5.6	"
C_3H_7	6.9	"
C_4H_9	8.1	"
C_5H_{11}	9.4	"
C_5H_{11}	9.4	Channel
C_6H_{13}	10.7	"
C_7H_{15}	11.9	"
C_8H_{17}	13.2	"
$C_{10}H_{21}$	15.7	"
$C_{12}H_{25}$	18.2	"
$C_{16}H_{33}$	23.2	"
$C_{18}H_{37}$	25.7	"

TABLE 3-5. ADDUCTS OF TRI-o-THYMOTIDE WITH UNBRANCHED
MOLECULES[156] (*Continued*)

Included Molecule (A) R·OH, Where R =		Calc. Length of Included Molecule in Extended Form in (Å)	Structure Types
(B) R·X			
R	X		
CH_3	Br	5.9	Cavity
CH_3	I	6.3	"
C_2H_5	Br	6.8	"
C_2H_5	I	7.1	"
C_3H_7	Br (A)	8.0	"
C_3H_7	Br (B)	8.0	"
C_3H_7	I	8.4	"
C_4H_9	Br	9.3	"
C_4H_9	I	9.6	Channel
C_5H_{11}	Br	10.5	"
C_5H_{11}	I	10.9	"
C_6H_{13}	Br	11.8	"
C_7H_{15}	Br	13.0	"
C_7H_{15}	I	13.4	"
C_8H_{17}	Br	14.3	"
C_8H_{17}	I (A)	14.7	"
C_8H_{17}	I (B)	14.7	"
$C_{16}H_{33}$	Br	24.4	"
$C_{16}H_{33}$	I	24.7	"
$C_{18}H_{37}$	Br	26.9	"
$C_{18}H_{37}$	I (A)	27.2	"
$C_{18}H_{37}$	I (B)	27.2	"

(C) X·$[CH_2]_n$·X			
n	X		
1	Br	7.0	Cavity
1	I	7.7	"
2	Br	8.3	"

TABLE 3-5. ADDUCTS OF TRI-*o*-THYMOTIDE WITH UNBRANCHED
MOLECULES[156] (*Continued*)

Included Molecule (A) R·OH, Where R = (C) X·[CH₂[ₙ·X (cont'd.)		Calc. Length of Included Molecule in Extended Form in (Å)	Structure Types
n	X		
3	Br (A)	9.5	Cavity
3	Br (B)	9.5	"
6	I	14.0	Channel
(D) ROR′			
R	R′		
C_2H_5	C_2H_5	8.9	Cavity
CH_3	C_4H_9	10.1	Channel
C_2H_5	C_4H_9	11.4	"
(E) C_nH_{2n+2}			
C_5H_{12}		9.0	"
C_6H_{14}		10.3	"
(F)			
I_2		7.0	Cavity
$Hg(C_2H_5)_2$		9.8	Channel
(G)			
$C_2H_4I_2$	90% of cavities vacant	—	Cavity

When the compound is heated to 120°C, benzene is
evolved; furthermore some of the benzene is removed
by repeatedly washing with ether. The crystals, which
are tetragonal in shape, have a delicate purple color.
By flotation, their density was determined to be 1.58
g/cc. Crystals of the thiophene clathrate were found
to form a similar compound which decomposed readily.
Advantage has been taken of this difference in the

properties of these clathrates of benzene and thio-phene, and they will be discussed later.

The chemistry of the clathrate compounds of cyclo-veratril warrants further elucidation. Caglioti and his

TABLE 3-6. ADDUCTS OF TRI-o-THYMOTIDE WITH BRANCHED MOLECULES[156]

Included Molecule (A) CORR′		Calc. Length of Included Molecule in Extended Form in (Å)	Structure Type
R	R′		
CH_3	CH_3	6.5	Cavity
C_2H_5	C_2H_5	9.0	"
A tetraketone*		49.2	Channel
(B) R·CO_2R′			
R	R′		
H	n-C_3H_7	9.5	Cavity
n-$C_{12}H_{25}$	CH_3	20.2	Channel
(C) CH_3·CHRX			
R	X		
C_2H_5	Br	8.0	Cavity
C_6H_{13}	OH	11.9	Channel
C_6H_{13}	Br (A)	13.0	"
C_6H_{13}	Br (B)	13.0	"

*CH_3·$[CH_2]_7$·CO·CH_2·CO·$[CH_2]_7$·CO·CH_2·CO·$[CH_2]_7$·CH_3.

co-workers[40,43,109] pointed out one particularly inter-esting observation made in the course of their studies on the structure of these clathrates. They compared the infrared spectra of many of the cycloveratril clath-rates and noted that besides the negligible contribu-

TABLE 3-7. THERMODYNAMIC DATA AND LATTICE CONSTANTS
OF SOME HYDRATES[299]

Solute (in order of increasing bp)	Dissociation Pressure at 0°C	Max. Temp. at Which Hydrates Exist, °C	Heat of Formation from Pure Water and Gas at 0°C kcal/Mole Solute	Lattice Constant, A
Ar	95.5 atm	No maximum exists	—	—
CH_4	26.0 atm	No maximum exists	14.5	—
Kr	14.5 atm	No maximum exists	13.9 ± 0.5	—
Xe	1.15 atm	No maximum exists	16.7 ± 0.5	12.0
C_2H_4	5.44 atm	No maximum exists	15.0	—
C_2H_6	5.2 atm	14.5	16.3	—
N_2O	10 atm	12	14.7	12.03
C_2H_2	5.7 atm	16	15	—
CO_2	12.47 atm	10.20	14.4	12.07
H_2S	698 mm	29.5	14.8	12.02
Cl_2	252 mm	28.7	16.0	12.03
CH_3Cl	311 mm	21	18.1	12.00
SO_2	297 mm	12.1	16.6	11.97
CH_3Br	187 mm	14.5	19.5	12.09
CH_3SH	239 mm	12	16.6	12.12
Br_2	43.90 mm	5.81	20.83	12.1
C_3H_8	1.74 atm	5.69	32	17.40
$CHCl_2F$	115 mm	8.61	32.7	—
C_2H_5Cl	201 mm	4.8	31.9	17.30
CH_2Cl_2	116 mm	1.7	29	17.33
CH_3I	74 mm	4.3	31.4	17.14
$CHCl_3$	50 mm	1.6	31	17.33

tion of the enclathrated molecules, which are present
in relatively small percentages by weight, the spectra
may be divided into α and β groups. This, they propose, may indicate two different types of crystal structure as in the tri-o-thymotide.

Studies on specific properties of clathrates, both as solids and in solution, have not been systematically pursued. Thermodynamic considerations[298,299], thermal decomposition, infrared investigations, and heats of formation are some of the areas in which work has been done.

The energies of interaction between the enclosed molecules and their hydroquinone cages have been discussed by Evans and Richards[88,89] who report that the forces acting upon an enclosed molecule can be roughly classified as:

(1) London dispersion forces.

(2) Dipole-induced dipole forces.

(3) Dipole-dipole forces.

(4) Repulsive forces and any loss of energy of the crystal lattice due to distortion by these forces.

The following approximate expression for the potential energy, V, of two molecules was derived by London[161]:

$$V = \frac{h v_1 h v_2}{h v_1 + h v_2} \frac{a_1 a_2}{r^6}$$

Theoretically the molecules should be spherically symmetrical and at a distance, r, apart. The characteristic frequencies, v_1 and v_2, of the two molecules are obtained from refractive index data or from the casual relationship, $hv = I$, where I is the ionization potential. The respective polarizabilities of the molecules are symbolized as a_1 and a_2. The London expression is of little value when applied to molecules which deviate from spherical symmetry as hydroquinone does. However, for small enclosed molecules such as Ar, O_2, N_2 and HCl the values of r will be approximately the same in each case so that potential energy will be proportional to the product of the polarizability of the enclosed molecule and some function (approximately the square root) of hv for the molecule. Variations of hv amogn different enclosed molecules will be much less important than the variations in the polarizability; accordingly the dispersion forces will be approximately proportional to the polarizability of the enclosed molecule.

As for the other forces listed, the dipole-induced dipole forces are caused mainly by the polar C-O and O-H bonds and will be directly proportional to the polarizability of the enclosed molecules. The dipole-dipole forces are absent in the hydroquinone clathrate compounds of Ar, O_2, and N_2 and are probably small in the hydroquinone-HCl clathrate. The magnitude of the repulsion forces will increase rapidly with a growth in size, or to a rough approximation, the polarizability of the enclosed molecule.

In the earliest studies on the free energy of formation the value of $-\Delta G$ of a β-hydroquinone clathrate was found by application of the relationship:

$$-\Delta G = -\Delta H + T\Delta S$$

Here ΔS is the change in entropy in the reaction:

$$\underset{\text{Solid } \beta\text{-hydroquinone}}{3 \; C_6H_4(OH)_2} \; + \; \underset{\substack{\text{Gaseous} \\ \text{molecule}}}{M} \; = \; \underset{\text{Clathrate compound}}{3 \; C_6H_4(OH)_2 \cdot M}$$

Evans and Richards[88] observed that if the β-hydroquinone lattice was undisturbed on formation of the clathrate compound, ΔS was equal to the difference in entropy of the molecule, M, when in the gas phase and when enclosed in the β-hydroquinone cage. In general, the entropy change was large and negative since the gaseous molecules lose all of their translational entropy, and if they are polyatomic, possibly some or all of their rotational entropy when the clathrate compound is formed. The enclosed molecules are, however, expected to gain vibrational entropy as a result of their oscillations in the β-hydroquinone cage.

Wynne-Jones and Anderson[316] have carried out vapor pressure studies on the hydroquinone clathrate compounds of sulfur dioxide and of methanol. They found that reversible vapor pressures are obtained on heating the clathrates, and free energies of formation can be derived from the equilibrium data.

Van der Waals and Platteeuw[300] have derived the thermodynamic properties of clathrates from what they refer to as a simple model which corresponds to the three-dimensional generalization of ideal localized adsorption. Certain basic assumptions were essential for their treatment, and the system consisted of the three phases: (1) clathrate, (2) non-clathrate modification of the host component, (3) free nonpolar gas. Statistical theory was applied to the study of the thermodynamic properties of, for example, the metastable host lattice, relative to the stable α-modification of hydroquinone, Table 3-8. Here the difference between α- and β-modifications $(\beta - \alpha)$ are given where $\Delta\mu$

represents the change in chemical potential, $\Delta\mu$ denotes the difference between molar heats of formation, and ΔV indicates the difference between molar volumes.

TABLE 3-8. THERMODYNAMIC PROPERTIES OF THE
METASTABLE HOST LATTICE, RELATIVE TO THE
STABLE α-MODIFICATION[299]

Host Lattice	$\Delta\mu$ kcal/mole	ΔH kcal/mole	ΔV ml/mole	V ml/mole
Hydroquinone, 25°C	0.082	0.16	4.6	82.8
Structure I	0.167	0	3.0	
Hydrates, 0°C				19.6
Structure II	0.19	—	3.4	

The better known clathrates—that is, the hydroquinone clathrates and the gas hydrate clathrates were explicitly chosen for study. Tabulations of data resulting from the statistical theory calculations are given in Table 3-9 where the equilibrium pressures of some

TABLE 3-9. EQUILIBRIUM PRESSURES OF HYDROQUINONE
CLATHRATES AT 25°C[299]

	P_k in atm*	
Solute	Calc.	Obs.
Argon	3.4	3.4
Krypton	0.4	0.4
Xenon	0.06	—
Methane	0.8	—
Nitrogen	5.2	5.8
Oxygen	2.6	—
HCl	0.02	$\simeq$ 0.01

* P_k is the pressure of solute molecules.

hydroquinone clathrates at 25°C, both as calculated and as observed are listed; furthermore Table 3-10 shows dissociation pressures of the gas hydrate clathrate, observed and calculated. Table 3-11 gives the energies of formation of some of the hydroquinone clathrates as calculated by van der Waals and Platteeuw[299] and as observed by Evans and Richards[88,89].

TABLE 3-10. DISSOCIATION PRESSURES OF GAS HYDRATES AT 273°K[299]

Hydrate Former	Dissociation Pressure (atm)	
	Obs.	Calc.
Argon	95.5	95.5
Krypton	14.5	15.4
Xenon	1.15	1.0
Methane	26	19.0
CF$_4$	$\simeq$1	1.6
Ethane	5.2	1.1
Ethylene	5.44	0.5
Oxygen	—	63
Nitrogen	—	90

TABLE 3-11. ENERGIES OF FORMATION OF HYDROQUINONE CLATHRATES[299]

Solute	Energy of Formation $\Delta*U$ in kcal*	
	Cal.	Obs.
Argon	−4.5	−5.4
Krypton	−6.1	—
Xenon	−8.0	—
Methane	−5.9	—
Nitrogen	−4.5	−5.2
Oxygen	−4.8	−4.9
HCl	−7.6	−8.6

* $\Delta*U$ is the energy of formation of the clathrate from β-hydroquinone and one mole of the gaseous solute at constant volume and 25°C.

Heterogeneous equilibria studies of binary systems of hydroquinone-rare gas, hydroquinone-methane, gas hydrates of Structure I and Structure II, and of ternary systems of the gas hydrates are also reported in full by van der Waals and Platteeuw[299]. Although this work will not be considered in detail here, it might be well to point out that as a result of part of the study further investigations were undertaken to clarify the picture of double hydrates versus mixed hydrates. Platteeuw and van der Waals definitely demonstrated the lack of distinction between the two[197,198,199]; they reported both types of hydrates to be solutions of two volatile solutes in a hydrate lattice. Wilcox and his associates[311] investigated the hydrocarbon gas hydrates.

Van der Waals[297] recently observed that it is not strictly possible to write the potential energy of enclathrated molecules as the sum of the values of the positional and orientational coordinates. The rotational contribution to the free energy will depend on the vibrational state. "This latter state corresponds," he says, "to the rattling of the molecule in its cage." Evidence for this loss of orientational freedom of polyatomic molecules in a clathrate is clearly shown by their smaller entropy of enclathration relative to that of monatomic gases.

In order to calculate the heats of formation of the clathrate compounds from α-hydroquinone Evans and Richards[89] report that it is necessary to know the heats of solution of the trapped compounds. These data are available[268], and some calorimetric measurements have been reported. Measurement of the thermal dissociation of clathrate compounds is difficult because the variations in the proportions of spaces which are occupied by the guest components in the various host frameworks are notable. Powell[215] reported the findings of Leech and Richards who were able to obtain reproducible results with the hydroquinone-hydrogen chloride clathrate. From the pressures at two different temperatures the heat content change, ΔH, in the exothermic reaction:

$$3 \; C_6H_4(OH)_2 + HCl \rightarrow \text{clathrate}$$
$$\textit{Solid } \beta\textit{-hydroquinone}$$

was found to be -10.1 kcal/mole. This value agrees fairly well with the value of -9.2 kcal/mole which was determined by Evans and Richards[89]. Table 3-12 gives the energies of interaction (heat evolved) of the gaseous enclosed molecules with the β-hydroquinone cage. These approximate the values for the gas hydrates which were measured by de Forcrand[98] and for the phenol clathrates which were measured by Nikitin and Kovalskaya[183].

TABLE 3-12

$-\Delta H$ per mole of Included Gas, Where $-\Delta H$ is the Heat Evolved in the Following Reaction at Constant Pressure:

$$3 \; \beta\text{-hydroquinone} + x\text{A} \rightarrow \text{clathrate}[299]$$

Ar	6.0 kcal
O_2	5.5
N_2	5.8
HCl	9.2
HBr	10.3
CH_3OH	11.0
$H \cdot COOH$	12.2

Dryden and Meakins[85] have investigated the extent of rotation of the enclathrated molecules in their hydroquinone cages. The rotation of the enclathrated molecules is shown by their dielectric properties. The enhancement in relative permittivity was found to be related to the dipole moments of the enclosed polar molecules. In Table 3-13 the values of the relative

TABLE 3-13. RELATIVE PERMITTIVITY[85]

Hydroquinone Compound	Dipole Moment of Polar Molecule (in D units)	ϵ' at 50 kc/s	ϵ' at 8,600 mc/s	ϵ'' at 8,600 mc/s
Hydroquinone cryst. from alcohol	—	2.9	—	—
Hydroquinone cryst. from water	—	2.8	2.8	<0.002
Clathrate compound with:				
Methanol	1.66	4.6	4.6	0.14
Hydrogen sulfide	1.1	3.4	3.2	<0.002
Hydrogen cyanide	2.6–3.0	9.2	8.2	0.57
Methyl cyanide	3.4	3.1	3.1	<0.003
Sulfur dioxide	1.7	3.9	3.7	0.015

permittivity, ϵ', listed at 50 kc/s, are those obtained after the low frequency absorption has decreased to such an extent that the relative permittivity has reached a constant value. The clathrate compounds have been shown to give larger values of ϵ' than the hydroquinone itself. The first three compounds given in the table show the enhancement of the relative permittivity to be nearly proportional to the square of the dipole moments of the polar molecules, which indicates that it is the orientation of these molecules in the structural cavities which results in the enhancement of ϵ'. Although the dipole moment of methyl cyanide is larger than that of any of the other polar compounds tested, its clathrate compound with hydroquinone showed only a small enhancement of the relative permittivity. This could be the result of the larger size of the methyl cyanide molecules, compared to the other compounds, which reduces their freedom of orientation in the crystal lattice. The anisotropy in dielectric properties shows clearly that enclathrated methyl cyanide molecules cannot rotate about axes perpendicular to the c direction of the hydroquinone-methyl cyanide crystal.

Clathrates are useful as compounds by means of which the susceptibilities of the "free" molecules of certain gases may be studied below temperatures at which the gases normally liquefy. Cooke and others[56,57,90] studied the magnetic susceptibility of oxygen in its hydroquinone clathrate cage and found that above 2°K the magnetic susceptibility of the enclathrated oxygen molecule was that calculated for a gas of non-interacting molecules. Below 2°K there was an appreciable departure from the "free gas" behavior. They concluded that the interaction of the oxygen molecules with the cages enclosing them is sufficient to affect their rotational freedom at temperatures in the liquid helium range. In a later paper Meyer and his associates[169] working below 2°K and as low as 0.25°K reported strong magnetic measurement evidence that the oxygen molecule in the hydroquinone cage is subject to a potential barrier, rather than being free. They also observed the absence of the ordinary resonance of the oxygen molecule in the clathrate, also indicating a lack of freedom.

Those double hydrates having the general formula, $A \cdot 2B \cdot 17 H_2O$, in which A may be acetone, methylene dichloride, chloroform, or carbon tetrachloride, and B may be argon, krypton, or xenon have been studied and reported on by von Stackelberg and Jahns[283]. Table 3-14 gives the temperatures, in °C, at which their decomposition pressure is 1 atm, moreover their stability increases from argon, to krypton, to xenon.

TABLE 3-14. DOUBLE HYDRATES: THE TEMPERATURES, °C,
AT WHICH THE DECOMPOSITION PRESSURE IS 1 ATM[304]

| Inert Gas | Organic Liquid | | | |
	Acetone	Methylene Dichloride	Chloroform	Carbon Tetrachloride
Argon	−8.0	−7.0	−4.8	−1.6
Krypton	−5.0	+6.2	+9.0	+11.3
Xenon	+3.0	+8.6	+10.9	+13.7

It was suggested by Aynsley, Campbell, and Dodd[11] that the rate determining step in the thermal decomposition of the benzene-monamminenickel(II) cyanide clathrate is the release of benzene from the cage to the surface. From their investigations they conclude that diffusion within the crystal lattice is comparatively easy.

Hart and Smith[117] described the stabilizing influence of p-xylene on tetra-(4-methylpyridine)-nickel dithiocyanate and gave the heat of formation of the clathrate and other properties. They, too, observed both the lack of any odor of the guest molecule, xylene, attached to the clathrate, and the ease with which the trapped molecule was released by dissolving and consequently destroying the clathrate in hydrochloric acid.

By means of nuclear magnetic resonance it is possible to tell whether a molecule or group is performing a rotational motion. Also, the nature of the rotational motion can usually be established, and a determination of the temperature-dependence of the rate of motion may be made[1]. Gilson and McDowell[111] undertook a nuclear magnetic resonance study of the molecular motion of enclathrated compounds in order to secure more information on the trapped compound. Though they report "enclathrated" compounds their work was with the thiourea cyclohexane inclusion compound which may not satisfy our definition of a true clathrate. It is of interest, however, that they found the normal rotations of the cyclohexane molecule at 25°C to be greatly restricted.

Parsonage and Staveley[190] report the measurement of the heat capacity, C_v, from about 13°K to about 273°K of a number of the hydroquinone clathrate compounds. The amount of argon enclathrated in the hydroquinone cages varied from approximately 20 to 80 per cent. This method of investigating the motion of ions or molecules in a lattice consists in an analysis of the heat capacity of the solid since the contribution to the heat capacity will, in general, differ according to whether the particles are freely rotating or executing torsional oscillations. The hydroquinone clathrates make it possible to study the behavior of molecules trapped individually in almost spherical cells[288].

Schaeffer and co-workers[243,245] pioneered in the work of selective clathration using Werner complexes. Since their first reports they have carried on a tremendous amount of work on petroleum mixtures, much of which is to be found described in the patent literature[51,242,244,246—253]. Kobe and Domask[145] surveyed the early research on urea adducts which analogously employed extractive crystallization in the separation of petroleum products.

TABLE 3-15. SEPARATION OF AROMATIC HYDROCARBON MIXTURES C_9 THROUGH C_{10} WITH Ni(4-METHYL-PYRIDINE)$_4$(SCN)$_2$[243]

Hydrocarbon Mixture	Sample	Analyses of Sample, Volume %		
		p-Isomer	m-Isomer	o-Isomer
Ethyltoluenes	Feed	33.4	47.3	19.0
	Crystals	58.4	25.1	16.5
	Filtrate	28.2	51.6	20.2
Cymenes	Feed	50.0	14.7	35.3
	Crystals	69.0	9.0	22.0
	Filtrate	35.6	13.8	50.6
Diethylbenzenes	Feed	15.7	71.4	12.9
	Crystals	29.3	67.4	3.3
	Filtrate	13.0	75.5	11.5

Tables 3-15 and 3-16 show feed mixture separation results which indicate some of the factors affecting the selective clathrate forming ability of the complex, Ni(4-methylpyridine)$_4$(SCN)$_2$, with respect to the size and the position of substitution of various functional groups on disubstituted benzene isomers. Tables 3-17 to 3-23 give the results of some of Schaeffer's work[245] on the separation and purification of organic compounds by means of their selective clathration from feed mixtures with other inorganic complex compounds. These applications have all been made in petroleum research. The "solution technique" referred to in the tables is described in Ch. 4.

TABLE 3-16. SEPARATION OF DISUBSTITUTED BENZENE
ISOMER MIXTURES WITH Ni(4-METHYLPYRIDINE)$_4$
(SCN)$_2$[243]

Isomer Mixture	Sample	Analyses of Samples, Weight %		
		p-Isomer	o-Isomer	m-Isomer
Chlorotoluenes	Feed	50.2	45.0	4.8
	Washed crystals	91.4	7.8	0.8
	Filtrate	38.6	56.7	4.7
Dichlorobenzenes	Feed	52.8	47.2	0
	Washed crystals	93.0	7.0	—
	Filtrate	37.5	62.5	—
Toluidines	Feed	49.1	50.9	0
	Washed crystals	68.4	31.6	—
Nitrotoluenes	Feed	50.0	50.0	0
	Washed crystals	73.5	26.5	—
	Filtrate	47.6	52.4	—
Methylanisoles	Feed	52.2	47.8	—
	Washed crystals	94.4	5.6	—
	Filtrate	39.3	60.7	—
Xylenes	Feed	26.9	22.2	50.7
	Washed crystals	84.2	3.5	12.3
	Filtrate	8.8	29.0	62.1

Radzitsky and Hanotier[8,228] have completed an extensive investigation on no less than 27 complexes of the general formula [Ni(SCN)$_2$ (primary substituted benzylamine)$_4$]. The thermal dissociations of several of the clathrates of these complexes have been investigated. Their selective nature is very well exemplified by the data given in Tables 3-24 and 3-25. Several

TABLE 3-17. SEPARATION OF p-XYLENE[245]

Complex[a]	Type of Contacting[b,c]	Wt. Ratios		Solvent or Thinner	Vol. % p-Xylene in Hydrocarbons from		
		Complex/Xylene	Solvent or Thinner/Complex		Feed	Crystals	Filtrate
Ni(4-mepy)$_4$(SCN)$_2$	Soln.	2.0	2.50	20% 4-Methylpyridine, 80% methyl cellosolve	19.4	50.0	4.9
Ni(4-etpy)$_4$(SCN)$_2$	Susp.	0.58	1.72	Excess xylene	22.3	43.9	19.7
Ni(4-vipy)$_4$(SCN)$_2$	Soln.	1.0	3.0	Chloroform	21.2	31.7	—
Co(4-mepy)$_4$(SCN)$_2$	Soln.	1.75	3.3	50% Butyl cellosolve, 50% methyl cellosolve	22.6	64.2	6.6
Mn(4-etpy)$_4$(SCN)$_2$	Susp.	0.28	3.5	Excess xylene	22.0	36.0	21.5
Mn(4-etpy)$_4$(SCN)$_2$	Soln.	2.0	2.5	20% 4-Ethylpyridine, 80% butyl cellosolve	19.4	38.8	8.0
Fe(4-etpy)$_4$(SCN)$_2$	Susp.	0.29	3.4	Excess xylene	23.0	46.5	20.5
Fe(4-mepy)$_4$(SCN)$_2$	Susp.	0.46	2.18	Excess xylene	20.2	31.7	17.5

a Abbreviations same as Table 2-4.
b Soln. = solution.
c Susp. = suspension.

TABLE 3-18. SEPARATION[a] OF C₈ AROMATIC ISOMERS BY SOLUTION[b,c] TECHNIQUE[245]

Complex[d]	C₈ Aromatic Clathrated	Wt. Ratio of Complex/Aromatics	Wt. Ratio of Complex/Excess Base[e]	Recovery, %	Clathrate C₈ Aromatic Comp.				Reject C₈ Aromatic Compn.			
					para	meta	ortho	Ethylbenzene	para	meta	ortho	Ethylbenzene
Ni(3-NH₂py)₄(SCN)₂	p-Xylene	0.75	1.5[e]	35.0	75.9	8.6	6.6	8.9	12.3	49.7	22.7	15.3
Ni(4-etpy)₄(formate)₂	o-Xylene	0.93	8.4	0.16	8.0	20.1	53.1	18.8	19.9	45.8	20.5	13.8
Mn(4-etpy)₄Cl₂	o-Xylene	0.75	3.0	0.032	14.9	39.4	37.9	7.8	19.4	46.5	19.2	14.9
Mn(4 etpy)₄(CN)₂	o-Xylene	1.75	16.	8.4	19.1	41.8	36.3	2.8	18.4	43.3	19.5	18.8
Mn(4-etpy)₄(CNO)₂	o-Xylene	1.75	16.	0.52	19.3	43.8	25.8	11.2	19.6	45.7	19.8	14.9
Ni(3-et-4mepy)₄(SCN)₂	m-Xylene	0.46	0[f]	0.75	15.4	56.9	6.7	21.0	19.4	46.2	19.8	14.6
Ni(4-acpy)₄(SCN)₂	Ethylbenzene	0.47	20	22	11.5	23.5	10.4	54.6	—	—	—	—

[a] Feed: 19.9 vol. % p, 45.5 % m, 19.3 % o-xylene, and 15.3 % ethylbenzene. [b] Solvent: methyl cellosolve with excess base. [c] Base was same as the base in the complex unless otherwise noted. [d] Abbreviations same as Table 2-4. [e] Excess base was 4-methylpyridine. [f] No excess base was employed.

other compounds which can be enclathrated to form these complexes are: dimethoxybenzenes, alkylbenzoates, dimethylnaphthalenes, and indan. The investigators have made a number of interesting observations concerning clathrates. Generally speaking, only

TABLE 3-19. SEPARATION[a] OF AROMATIC HYDROCARBONS, C_6 THROUGH C_8 WITH $N_I(4\text{-METHYLPYRIDINE})_4(SCN)_2$[245]

| Hydrocarbon Feed Mixture | Sample | Analyses of Sample, Vol. % | | | | Wt. Ratio[b] Clathrate Former to p-Xylene |
		p-Xylene	o-Xylene	Toluene	Benzene	
p-Xylene-toluene	Feed	48.7		51.3		5.8
	Crystals	64.5		35.5		
	Filtrate	35.8		64.2		
p-Xylene-benzene	Feed	47.9			52.1	
	Crystals	75.6			24.4	5.8
	Filtrate	33.4			66.6	
o-Xylene-benzene	Feed		55.1		44.9	
	Crystals		15.2		84.8	4.1[c]
	Filtrate		70.8		29.2	
o-Xylene-toluene	Feed		55.0	45.0		
	Crystals		21.1	78.9		4.1[c]
	Filtrate		64.9	35.1		
Benzene-toluene	Feed			49.4	50.6	
	Crystals			38.9	61.1	3.4[d]
	Filtrate			60.4	39.6	

[a] Solution technique; solvent 90 vol. % methyl cellosolve, 10 vol. % 4-methylpyridine. Weight ratio solvent/clathrate former = 2.0. [b] For initial solution. [c] Clathrate former to o-xylene. [d] Clathrate former to toluene.

compounds containing at least 1 aromatic ring are enclathrated. Very polar or reactive substituents on the aromatic ring must be avoided. An accumulation of polar groups makes the compounds less easily enclathrated; for example, dichlorobenzene is capable of being

TABLE 3-20. RECOVERY OF p-XYLENE FROM GASOLINE[245]

Type of Contacting	Gasoline	Wt. Ratio of Clathrate Former/p-Xylene	Sample	Aromatics Content of Gasoline, Vol. %	Xylenes Analyses,[b] Vol. %				Re-covery[c]
					p-Xylene	m-Xylene	o-Xylene	Ethyl-benzene	
Solution[a]	Reformed[d]	6.2	Feed	51.7	18.8	44.0	21.8	15.4	—
			Unwashed crystals		60.7	15.7	7.7	15.9	67.0
			Washed crystals		70.6	10.9	4.4	14.1	60.3
			Filtrate		8.0	48.8	25.5	17.7	31.2
Solution[a]	Reformed[d]	12.3	Feed	51.7	18.8	44.0	21.8	15.4	—
			Unwashed crystals		53.0	17.6	8.2	21.2	83.0
			Washed crystals		65.7	9.7	4.3	20.3	72.0
			Filtrate		3.9	54.9	27.6	13.6	12.1
Suspension[f]	Straight run[e]	10.0	Feed	14.3	13.8	44.1	21.1	16.0	—
			Unwashed crystals		55.3	15.3	4.6	24.8	69.0
			Filtrate		4.0	57.4	24.5	14.1	—

[a] Ni(4-methylpyridine)$_4$(SCN)$_2$ in 20 vol. % 4-methylpyridine, 80 % methyl cellosolve. Weight ratio solvent/complex = 2.0. [b] Of C$_8$ aromatic hydrocarbons, normalized to 100 %. [c] Volume of p-xylene charged as feed recovered in that sample. [d] Heart cut with overhead temperatures 130 to 145° inclusive, taken with 20 plates and 10 to 1 reflux ratio from a catalytically reformed gasoline prepared from a Western light straight-run gasoline stock. [e] Heart cut with overhead temperatures 125 to 151° inclusive, taken with 20 plates and 10 to 1 reflux ratio from a Western straight-run gasoline. [f] Thinner was 1 volume of isooctane per 2.2 volumes of gasoline.

TABLE 3-21. SEPARATION[a] OF AROMATIC HYDROCARBON MIXTURES, C_8 THROUGH C_{10} WITH Ni(4-METHYLPYRIDINE)$_4$(SCN)$_2$[245]

Hydrocarbon Feed Mixture	Sample	Analyses of Sample, Vol. %				Recovery	Wt. Ratio[b] Clathrate Former to p-Isomer
		p-Isomer	m-Isomer	o-Isomer	Ethylbenzene		
Ethyltoluenes	Feed	33.4	47.3	19.0	—	—	—
	Crystals	58.4	25.1	16.5	—	25.8	6.4
	Filtrate	28.2	51.6	20.2	—	74.2	
Cymenes	Feed	50.0	14.7	35.3	—	—	—
	Crystals	69.0	9.0	22.0	—	24.5	1.9
	Filtrate	35.6	13.8	50.6	—	75.5	
Diethylbenzenes	Feed	15.7	71.4	12.9	—	—	—
	Crystals	29.3	67.4	3.3	—	17.5	9.3
	Filtrate	13.0	75.5	11.5	—	82.5	
Xylenes	Feed	78.7	9.2	1.8	10.3	—	—
	Washed crystals	97.7	0.7	0.7	2.3	70.5	5.8
	Filtrate	46.7	25.9	2.2	25.2	29.5	
Xylenes	Feed	26.9	50.7	22.2	—	—	—
	Unwashed crystals	68.0	22.8	8.4	—	83.2	8.1
	Filtrate	8.8	62.1	29.0	—	16.7	
	Washed crystals	84.2	12.3	3.5	—	79.7	
	Wash filtrate	24.7	51.9	23.4	—	3.8	

[a] Solution technique; solvent 90 vol. % methyl Cellosolve, 10 vol. % methyl 4-methylpyridine. Weight ratio solvent/clathrate former = 2.0. [b] For initial solution.

TABLE 3-22. SEPARATION OF di-SUBSTITUTED BENZENE ISOMER MIXTURES WITH Ni(4-METHYLPYRIDINE)$_4$(SCN)$_2$[245]

Isomeric Mixture	Wt. ratio of Clathrate Former to p-isomer	Sample	Analyses of Samples, Wt. %			Recovery[a]
			p-Isomer	o-Isomer	m-Isomer	
Chlorotoluenes	7.67	Feed	50.2	45.0	4.8	—
		Washed crystals[b]	91.4	7.8	0.8	35
		Filtrate	38.6	56.7	4.7	65
Dichlorobenzenes	3.08	Feed	52.8	47.2	0	—
		Washed crystals[b]	93.0	7.0	—	34.8
		Filtrate	37.5	62.5	—	65.2
Toluidines	4.16	Feed	49.1	50.9	0	—
		Washed crystals[b]	68.4	31.6	—	10.1
Nitrotoluenes	3.47	Feed	50.0	50.0	0	—
		Washed crystals[b]	73.5	26.5	—	7.0
		Filtrate	47.6	52.4	—	93.0
Methylanisole	2.57	Feed	52.2	47.8	—	—
		Washed crystals[b]	94.4	5.6	—	25.5
		Filtrate	39.3	60.7	—	74.5

Solvent (vol. %), 10% 4-methylpyridine, 90% methyl cellosolve in all experiments.

$$\frac{\text{Solvent}}{\text{Clathrate former}} \text{ (weight ratio)} = 2.0 \text{ in all experiments.}$$

[a] Weight % of the p-isomer introduced as feed recovered in that phase. [b] Clathrate crystals were washed once with fresh solvent before recovering the clathrated product contained therein.

110

TABLE 3-23. SEPARATION OF POLYCYCLIC COMPOUNDS WITH Ni(4-METHYLPYRIDINE)$_4$(SCN)$_2$[245]

Type of Contacting	Feed		Sample	Analyses, Wt. %			Wt. Ratio, Clathrate Former to Compd. 1	Soln. Temp. °C	Filtration Temp. °C
	Compound 1	Compound 2		Compd. 1	Compd. 2	Recovery, %			
Solution[a]	Naphthalene	Diphenyl	Feed	48.6	51.4	—	3.0	108	25
			Washed crystals	85.6	14.4	83			
			Filtrate	14.8	85.2	17			
Solution[a]	1-Methylnaphthalene	2-Methylnaphthalene	Feed	58.3	41.7	—	2.6	105	21
			Washed crystals	81.3	18.7	43			
			Filtrate	45.5	54.5	57			
Solution[a]	Anthracene	Phenanthrene	Feed	33.3	66.7	—	10.0	94	25
			Washed crystals	97.9	2.1	—			
			Filtrate	20.2	79.8	—			
Solution[a]	Diphenyl oxide	Phenanthrene	Feed	54.1	45.9	—	3.3	81	30
			Washed crystals	83.7	16.3	—			
			Filtrate	50.8	49.2	—			
Suspension[b]	Naphthalene	Diphenyl	Feed	50.0	50.0	—	4.0	20	20
			Washed crystals	74.4	25.6	—			
			Filtrate	23.4	74.4	—			

ᵃ Solvent: 90 vol. % methyl cellosolve, 10 vol. % 4-methylpyridine. ᵇ n-Heptane as diluent.

TABLE 3-24. CLATHRATION OF XYLENES USING COMPLEXES OF THE TYPE $[Ni(SCN)_2(R_2C_6H_4CH(R_1)NH_2)_4]$[228]

| Amines | | Composition of Xylenes (wt %) in | | | | | | Cp | Cm | Selectivity |
| | | Feed | | | Clathrate | | | | | |
R_1	R_2	o-	m-	p-	o-	m-	p-			
Me	H	37.1	31.1	31.8	61.9	19.5	18.6	18.2	1.57	o-
Et	H	37.1	31.1	31.8	12.3	25.8	61.9	17.8	1.61	p-
Pr	H	37.1	31.1	31.8	22.9	7.5	69.6	11.3	1.06	p-
But	H	34.2	31.2	34.6	83.8	13.6	2.6	10.8	0.98	o-
isoBut	H	33.6	31.9	34.5	72.2	19.4	8.4	17.5		o-
Am	H	33.9	31.7	34.4	4.6	70.9	24.5	8.9	1.11	m-
Hex	H	33.9	31.7	34.4	12.4	79.4	8.2	8.9		m-
Oct	H	33.6	31.9	34.5	11.3	71.6	17.1	4.0		m-
Me	p-Me	34.2	30.1	35.7	60.0	11.2	28.8	13.8	1.18	o-
Me	o-Me	0	19.4	80.6	0	2.4	97.7	12.4	1.05	p-
Me	p-Et	37.1	31.1	31.8	78.1	18.4	3.5	9.3	0.98	o-
Me	p-iso-Prop	37.1	31.1	31.8	89.4	7.6	3.0	12.3	1.73	o-
Me	p-t-But	37.1	31.1	31.8	83.2	13.1	3.7	6.8	0.86	o-
Me	p-OCH$_3$	34.2	30.1	35.7	50.7	36.3	13.0	15.6	1.41	o- > m-
Me	p-F	35.8	31.4	32.8	33.3	27.2	39.5	11.1	1.54	p-
Me	p-Cl	34.2	30.1	35.7	26.4	26.4	47.2	17.7	1.71	p-
Me	o-Cl	35.8	31.4	32.8	36.5	20.0	43.8	9.3	0.93	p- > o-
Me	p-Br	34.2	30.1	35.7	4.8	27.3	67.9	9.8	1.03	p-
Me	p-I	35.8	31.4	32.8	37.9	22.9	39.2	15.3	2.17	p- > o-
Me	m-NO$_2$	35.8	31.4	32.8	21.9	14.0	64.1	9.1	0.89	p-
Prop	p-Me	33.9	31.7	34.4	57.3	31.3	11.4	8.9	0.96	o-
Prop	p-Br	34.8	31.5	33.7	63.2	28.5	8.3	7.7	1.02	o-
isoBut	p-Br	33.9	31.7	34.4	85.5	11.1	3.4	8.7	1.08	o-

Cp = % by weight of enclathrated xylenes in the clathrate. Cm = mole of enclathrated xylenes per mole of four base complex (clathrates often contain two base complex and some water).

enclathrated at the temperature of an ice bath, but trichlorobenzene is not. Also, an accumulation of bulky groups retards clathration; for example, ethyl*iso*propylbenzene is enclathrated but di*iso*propylbenzene is not.

TABLE 3-25. CLATHRATION OF METHYLNAPHTHALENES USING
COMPLEXES OF THE TYPE
$[Ni(SCN)_2(R_2C_6H_4CH(R_1)NH_2)_4]^{228}$

Amines		Composition of Methyl-naphthalenes in Weight % in the Clathrate		Cp	Cm	Selec-tivity
R_1	R_2	Feed α = 55.5	β = 44.5			
Me	*p*-cyclo-Hex	69.9	30.1	29.3	2.97	α-
H	*p*-Me	84.2	15.8	14.1	0.82	α-
H	*p*-Br	56.7	48.3	7.6	0.55	α-
H	*p*-N(CH_3)_2	59.4	40.6	29.3	2.33	α-

(Cp and Cm as in Table 3-24)

According to Radzitzky and Hanotier several generalizations with reference to their compounds may be made. They maintain that the stability of the clathrates which they prepared are related to both electronic and steric factors. Moreover they believe that electronic factors certainly play a part as proven by the interaction between the aromatic rings of the amine and of the enclathrated compound, and that this interaction is of the pi-complex type, that is, the aromatic ring of the amine is the electron acceptor and the aromatic ring of the enclathrated compound is the electron donor. Only aromatic compounds can be enclathrated in their complexes; cyclic compounds derived from cyclohexane or decaline cannot be. Also, aromatic compounds carrying electronegative groups are less easily enclathrated than compounds having electropositive groups of roughly the same size. The lack of any observable color change is evidence that whatever interaction does occur is certainly weaker than in true pi-complexes. When the ring substituents become increasingly large, the steric factors become more important, nevertheless, they conclude, much work remains to be done before an adequate mechanism of enclathration can be proposed.

The selectivity of the complexes formed between nickel thiocyanate and substituted primary benzylamines on clathration is quite remarkable. Some general tendencies were drawn up in which both the nature of the amine and the nature of the enclathrated compound were shown to be important. As seen from Table 3-24 the isomers of xylene may be enclathrated selectively by different complexes. On the other hand, the complex [Ni(SCN)$_2$(α-propylbenzylamine)$_4$] will enclathrate selectively each of the three isomers (*ortho-*, *meta-*, and *para-*) of three different aromatic compounds. When the aromatic ring of the enclathrated component has two large groups, the *ortho-* isomer is best enclathrated. The selectivity order of any of these complexes with ethyl*iso*propylbenzene is *ortho-* > *meta-* > *para-*. With trialkylbenzenes the same holds true, that is, the order is 1,2,3, > 1,2,4, > 1,3,5. With symmetrical trisubstituted benzenes steric hindrance is such that practically no enclathration occurs. When the aromatic ring of the enclathrated compound has two relatively small substituents, the electronic interactions are expected to be more significant.

Three selectivity rules which were established for the enclathration of xylenes by complexes formed with *meta-* or *para-* substituted α-methylbenzylamine are:

(1) Complexes in which the amine has a substituent on the *meta-* or *para-* position which gives a negative inducing effect (F^-, Cl^-, Br^-, I^-, NO_2) display *para-* selectivity.

(2) Complexes in which the amine has a substituent which gives a positive inducing effect (CH_3, C_2H_5, etc.) display *ortho-* selectivity.

(3) The changing selectivities for xylenes when the *alpha* alkyl group of the amine goes from the methyl to the octyl group is due to steric factors.

Some preliminary work has been done on the infrared spectra of clathrate compounds. Besides that of Caglioti which was mentioned earlier in this chapter, Hexter and Goldfarb[123] have determined spectral evidence that rotation of the carbon dioxide molecule in its hydroquinone cage is not free. They have also studied the hydroquinone clathrate compounds of hydrogen chloride, hydrogen sulfide and sulfur dioxide. Radzitsky[229] has initiated a series of investigations on the infrared spectra of his [Ni(SCN)$_2$(primary substituted benzylamine)$_4$] complexes. It is too soon to draw any conclusions from his work though it promises to be very interesting.

Other studies which have recently appeared in the

literature include the epitaxy studies of clathrates by Ferroni and Cocchi[94] and the polymerization of isoprene in several clathrate complexes by means of γ-radiation. The polymerization studies were carried out in the molecular complexes based on derivatives of 4,4'-dihydroxy-triphenylmethane[18].

CHAPTER 4

Preparation of
Clathrate Compounds

In his first report on clathrate compounds, Powell described their modes of formation, from which it appears to be essential that the molecules of host and the molecules of guest components be present in solution in a favorable ratio. On crystallization, the host molecules will slowly aggregate to build a framework around their guest molecules; consequently a high concentration of the guest component is an important factor in clathrate formation. Physical methods such as high pressure in the case of gases may be used to bring about the maximum ratio of guest to host in the clathrate compound.

When the host is soluble in the guest component, the preparation may be expected to proceed without difficulty to the formation of a clathrate compound in which the ratio of host to guest molecules is a stoichiometric one, or approximately so. When a solvent common to both components must be used, some problems may be encountered; for example, when the guest component concentration is low, both slow crystallization and stirring are advised. These precautions will ensure adequate concentration of the guest component at the site of crystallization.

A unique way of obtaining a clathrate compound of some substances which might not normally enclathrate has been suggested by Powell[204]. It involves the enclathration of molecules which can be decomposed within the cages. Two factors, of course, must be present, namely: (1) the enclathrated component must be capable of decomposition, and (2) the cage component must be stable under the decomposition conditions. Decomposition by heat, ultraviolet light, x-ray, radiation, or some similar method may prove to be particularly applicable.

Other characteristics which are to be remembered when clathrate compounds are prepared are the sizes and shapes of both host and guest components. For any given cage the type of molecule to be enclosed will not be determined as much by its chemical nature as by its size and shape. There will, of necessity, be both lower and upper limits of size. The enclosing component must have an open structure which is rigid but in which the directed linkages which hold the molecules together in the crystals have sufficient extension of the groups to produce usefully large cavities.

The numerous and diverse methods by means of which clathrate compounds may be formed vary from extremely simple procedures to those which are more involved. Representative preparations of each type of clathrate will illustrate this diversity. Examples of the preparation of the many different groups of clathrate compounds as described in the literature are given here.

The Hydroquinone Clathrates

The early descriptions of the preparation of hydroquinone clathrates by Palin and Powell[188] indicate that their formation is relatively simple. The preparations are as follows:

(a) The hydroquinone-sulfur dioxide clathrate may be formed by passing a steady stream of sulfur dioxide through a saturated aqueous solution of hydroquinone at room temperature. The clathrate compound crystallizes slowly from the solution.

(b) The hydroquinone-methanol clathrate may be prepared by crystallization from a solution of hydroquinone in methanol at ordinary temperatures.

(c) Methyl cyanide forms a clathrate with hydroquinone by crystallization, on cooling, from a warm solution of hydroquinone in methyl cyanide.

(d) The hydroquinone-formic acid clathrate crystallizes, on cooling, from a warm saturated solution of hydroquinone in formic acid whose concentration exceeds 95 per cent. Any appreciable dilution of the formic acid with water results in the formation of α-hydroquinone.

(e) Carbon dioxide forms a hydroquinone clathrate with greater difficulty. About 2 grams of solid carbon dioxide is added to 10 ml of a saturated aqueous solution of hydroquinone (saturated at 40°C) contained in a Parr bomb. The bomb is heated to 50°C and then allowed to cool slowly to room temperature. After a short time the crystalline product separates.

(f) A hydroquinone-hydrogen chloride clathrate will crystallize from a saturated solution of hydroquinone in ether after saturation with hydrogen chloride at 20°C.

(g) The hydroquinone-hydrogen sulfide clathrate crystallizes from a saturated aqueous solution of hydroquinone which has also been saturated with hydrogen sulfide at 30°C.

(h) To form the hydroquinone-acetylene clathrate, acetylene is passed through a saturated solution of hydroquinone in ether.

(i) A clathrate of sulfur dioxide + methanol may be prepared by crystallization from a saturated solution of hydroquinone in methanol which has also been saturated with sulfur dioxide at 20°C.

(j) Sulfur dioxide + hydrogen chloride form a clathrate when sulfur dioxide and hydrogen chloride are passed into a saturated solution of hydroquinone in ether. As soon as precipitation starts, both gas streams are cut off and crystallization is allowed to continue slowly at room temperature.

The hydroquinone clathrates of the inert gases, argon, krypton, and xenon are prepared under special pressure conditions. In general, a saturated solution of hydroquinone in water at room temperature may be placed in a stainless-steel pressure vessel along with an excess of hydroquinone which is approximately equal to the weight of product desired. After the atmospheric gases are flushed from the reaction vessel, the inert gas is introduced and maintained under constant pressure. The mixture is heated in a water-bath and then allowed to cool slowly in order to control the rate of crystal formation. The excess hydroquinone should dissolve at the elevated temperature, and crystal formation should not occur until the final stages of cooling.

There is no strong interaction between the hydroquinone and an inert gas; therefore there is no spontaneous tendency for the latter to be included in the crystal such as might be assumed for polar compounds like hydrogen sulfide and sulfur dioxide. It is therefore necessary to control conditions so that an inert gas atom is available and in position at the surface of the growing crystal whenever hydroquinone molecules link to form a cage[275]. As the solubilities of the gases in water are low, this situation can be assured only by using fairly high pressures. In Powell's[209] work the gas pressures were 40, 20 and 14 atm for Ar, Kr, and Xe, respectively. The solubilities of the gases increase with increasing atomic weights.

The first preparation of a clathrate compound of hydroquinone with an inert gas was carried out by Powell and Guter[222]. Their method of preparation is as follows:

"A 0.7 gram sample of hydroquinone and 60 ml of benzene were placed in a stainless steel pressure vessel. Air was removed by pumping, and argon was introduced into the reaction vessel. The pressure of the spectroscopically pure argon was raised to 20 atm. The temperature of the solution, initially at 30°C, was raised to 87.5°C, and the vessel was then allowed to cool at an average rate of 1°C per three hours to 19.2°C."

Hydroquinone-argon crystals formed slowly. At a later date Powell[207] reported that the initial use of benzene resulted in a comparatively small yield, due to the low solubility of hydroquinone in benzene. In order to obviate this difficulty either ethanol or water was used. Methanol was avoided because of its tendency to form a clathrate compound. This improvement on the original method involved the use of 30 ml of a saturated aqueous solution of hydroquinone and argon under 40 atm of pressure. The hydroquinone-argon clathrate which formed was obtained in large single crystals in the form of hexagonal prisms with terminal rhombohedron faces. It corresponded in composition to the formula $3 C_6H_4(OH)_2 \cdot 0.8$ Ar. Some α-hydroquinone also formed as very thin needles, however separation was readily effected by hand picking.

Later the hydroquinone-krypton clathrate compound was prepared by placing 60 ml of a saturated aqueous solution of hydroquinone in a pressure vessel with a 2 g excess of hydroquinone. A pressure of 20 atm of krypton was applied from a cylinder of the gas, and the temperature was raised to 95°C in order to dissolve the additional hydroquinone. The solution was then allowed to cool for twelve hours and crystals of the hydroquinone-krypton clathrate formed. Some of these crystals were several millimeters in thickness. Also, some α-hydroquinone separated out, and a complete separation of the two could not be made. The composition of the clathrate which was determined is represented by the formula, $3 C_6H_4(OH)_2 \cdot 0.74$ Kr.

The preparation of the hydroquinone-xenon clathrate compound was like that of krypton; however, a pressure of only 14 atm was applied. Only very small crystals of a mixture were obtained from the aqueous solution. By solvent extraction, using carbon tetrachloride, the dense fraction of the mixture was isolated and found to contain 26 per cent xenon. The composition of this product corresponds to the formula, $3 C_6H_4(OH)_2 \cdot 0.88$ Xe. The colorless crystals appear quite stable. Like those of argon and krypton, they liberate the enclathrated inert gas when dissolved, or on heating.

The early reports on the preparations of the hydroquinone clathrates have been extended by more recent workers. Chleck and Ziegler[49,50] prepared the hydroquinone-krypton clathrate in which they used radioactive krypton as the guest component. They described the method as follows: "We place a sample of quinol (hydroquinone) in a pressure vessel, eliminate atmospheric gases and fill the apparatus with carrier-free krypton containing 5 per cent Kr[85], the form commonly available from Oak Ridge. The quinol is heated to slightly above its melting point (185°C) and then slowly cooled over a long time. High gas pressure and controlled cooling to prevent rapid crystal formation fulfill the requirements for good clathrating. Our maximum clathrating efficiency is obtained at 60 atm and a growth period of seventy-two hours. Clathrate compounds prepared by this method contain about 25 per cent of the theoretical maximum of krypton."

The maximum composition hydroquinone-krypton clathrate compound prepared by Powell has a 15.8 per cent krypton content, i. e., a composition corresponding to 3 $C_6H_4(OH)_2 \cdot 0.74$ Kr.

Peyronel and Barbieri[195] described the preparation of the hydroquinone clathrates of nitrous oxide, methane, monochloromethane, and of propane. They varied the pressures which they applied with the various compounds to be enclathrated. According to their method: "A solution of hydroquinone in ethanol saturated at 30°C was warmed in a stainless steel bomb at 35°C; the air was removed by repeated flushing with the gas and the bomb filled with the gas at the desired pressure. The solution was cooled from 35°C to 22°C in eight hours, and the pressure inside the bomb was kept constant during the cooling period." The clathrate compounds which they prepared were of compositions corresponding to the formulas given below at the pressures indicated:

3 $C_6H_4(OH)_2 \cdot CH_4$	at	100 atm
3 $C_6H_4(OH)_2 \cdot 0.75$ CH_3Cl	at	5 atm
3 $C_6H_4(OH)_2 \cdot 0.76$ N_2O	at	20 atm
3 $C_6H_4(OH)_2 \cdot 0.37$ C_3H_8	at	9 atm

They also report the clathrability of methane and nitrogen at 100 atm of pressure with approximately 1 molecule of guest in each 3 $C_6H_4(OH)_2$ cage.

The hydroquinone-oxygen clathrate compound was prepared by Evans and Richards[88] who used a hot concentrated solution of hydroquinone in air-free ethyl alcohol (later propanol was found to be the better solvent) in a "Monel"-metal pressure bomb into which oxygen was introduced and maintained at a pressure of from 25 to 40 atm. The mixture was allowed to cool slowly for twenty-four hours. Faintly yellow crystals which darkened on exposure to strong sunlight were obtained. The compound was of the composition indicated by a range of 0.4 to 0.5 O_2 to each 3 $C_6H_4(OH)_2$ cage.

Evans and Richards[89] also prepared the hydroquinone-nitric oxide clathrate compound. A warm saturated solution of hydroquinone in ethyl alcohol was boiled to remove dissolved air and subsequently poured into a stainless steel bomb. The bomb was evacuated with a rotatory pump and quickly cooled in liquid oxygen. Nitric oxide was passed through a previously evacuated train of traps to remove nitrogen dioxide and water and was allowed to condense in the bomb. A pressure of approximately 40 atm was maintained in the bomb at room temperature. After the bomb valve was closed, the bomb was removed from the liquid oxygen and finally immersed in hot water. It was shaken for some time to redissolve the hydroquinone; then it was allowed to cool slowly for twenty-four hours. The clathrate compound which formed contained amounts of nitric oxide which corresponded to about 50 per cent of the available space.

The hydroquinone-nitrogen clathrate compound was prepared by crystallization from an *n*-propyl alcohol solution of hydroquinone under a pressure of about 30 atm of nitrogen. A hot aqueous solution of hydroquinone treated with nitrogen under a pressure of only 20 atm on rapid cooling gave a different clathrate compound corresponding to the formula, 3 $C_6H_4(OH)_2 \cdot 0.08$ N_2, in which the cage component has the α-hydroquinone structure.

The Water Clathrates or Gas Hydrates

Many small molecules form stable crystals with water at low temperatures. The inert gas hydrates of Ar, Kr, and Xe are formed when water and the gas are brought together under high pressures at very low temperatures. They have been shown to be clathrate compounds[278–287]. All the original preparations of the hydrates date back many years[78,98,303]; however, a more recent method of preparation of the clathrate hydrate of chlorine, $Cl_2 \cdot 6H_2O$ was described by Pauling and Marsh[191]. "A length of 6 mm "Pyrex" tubing was drawn to a capillary at one end and connected to a tank of commercial chlorine. After thorough flushing, the capillary was sealed off, and the end was immersed in a dry-ice-acetone bath. When some chlorine had condensed in the capillary, a drop of water was admitted into the large end of the glass tube which was then sealed off. Alternate warming and cooling of the capillary permitted thorough mixing of the water and chlorine. Small pale-yellow crystals soon formed in the capillary and remained as the temperature rose to 0°C. A small amount of liquid chlorine also remained, showing the Cl_2 was in excess."

In a patented method for the purification of salt

water Donath[84] describes a method for the preparation of solid hydrates. According to his description solid hydrates may be formed by forcing gas under pressures of from 100 to 1000 lb/sq in gage, at from 40 to 75°F into salt water. At a constant pressure of 34 atm ethane forms a hydrate at about 57°F which can be separated from the solution and decomposed at 60 to 70°F. In another relatively new water purification process[6] a light hydrocarbon such as propane, or a halogenated propane, is mixed with sea water under reduced pressure (57 psig for propane) and at a reduced temperature (35°F). The gas combines with sea water to form a salt-free water clathrate compound. In the case of propane gas the compound has a composition represented by 1 mole of propane to 17 moles of water. The crystals may be separated from the brine and washed. At a temperature of 45°F and a pressure of 70 psig they yield potable water.

One of the more recent accounts of the preparation of gas and water clathrates is that of Waller[304] who reported the preparation of a number of new clathrate compounds of the inert gases. Hydrates were made under elevated pressures in a stainless steel vessel or at atmospheric pressure in glass. The gases were introduced into the reaction vessel under pressure. By allowing the gases to escape slowly while maintaining a constant pressure the mixtures were kept agitated. Argon at pressures up to 120 atm was taken directly from a cylinder. For higher pressures it was fed into a compressor.

Double hydrates were prepared using acetone, methylene dichloride, chloroform, or carbon tetrachloride as the third component. The compounds obtained were of the type described by von Stackelberg[280], having the formula, $A \cdot 2B \cdot 17H_2O$, where A is the organic component and B is the inert gas. The acetone compounds were prepared by cooling in a bath at approximately $-30°C$. The other compounds were prepared in a cooling bath at between $-5°$ and $-10°C$. To maintain a fine suspension of the halogenated methanes, about 0.01 per cent of sodium dodecylbenzene sulfonate was added to the water.

Argon compounds were prepared at pressures between 200 and 400 atm, krypton compounds at about 30 atm, and xenon compounds at atmospheric pressure. The xenon compounds were sufficiently stable to be formed simply by bubbling the gas through the appropriate solvent mixture, cooled to $0°C$. All of the krypton compounds, with the exception of the acetone compound, could be obtained in the same way. Those compounds which formed at atmospheric pressure had a low percentage of gas enclathrated. By increasing the pressures the percentage could be increased from as low as 20 per cent to nearly 100 per cent of the stoichiometrical amount. The clathrates of krypton and xenon with heavy water have also been prepared[113].

Von Stackelberg suggested certain criteria for the properties of organic compounds that are capable of hydrate formation. In particular, he suggested, they should not have strong van der Waals' forces; consequently their boiling points should be less that $60°C$.

Also, they should not exhibit strong hydrogen bonding and should generally be insoluble in water.

The Phenol Clathrates

Terres and Vollmer[292,293] first identified a product formed by phenol with hydrogen sulfide as $2 C_6H_5OH \cdot H_2S$. They obtained it during the course of studies on the solubilities of petroleum and tar constituents in liquid hydrogen sulfide. Nikitin[180,183], von Stackelberg[280,282], and their respective associates have studied the clathrates of phenol with such guest components as xenon, hydrogen chloride, hydrogen bromide, hydrogen iodide, hydrogen sulfide, hydrogen selenide, sulfur dioxide, carbon dioxide carbon disulfide, methyl bromide, dichloromethane, fluoroethylene, 1,1-difluoroethane, and carbon disulfide + air. The general procedures for the preparations of phenol clathrate compounds resemble those for the hydroquinone clathrates. Crystallization from solutions of phenol dissolved in the guest component or the introduction of the gas molecules under pressure are the accepted methods.

Nikitin prepared the compound, $2 C_6H_5OH \cdot Xe$, by evacuating a 5 ml U-tube and placing finely powdered and dried phenol in it. The tube was then cautiously filled with Xe at $-50°C$. Hydrogen sulfide was introduced, and the pressure was reduced to 25 to 30 mm. In the presence of crystal nuclei of $2 C_6H_5OH \cdot H_2S$ the reaction of Xe with phenol was initiated at a partial pressure of Xe of 1 atm at $-30°C$. He and his associates prepared and studied the mixed phenol clathrates of xenon, radon, hydrogen chloride, hydrogen bromide, water, sulfur dioxide, and carbon dioxide.

The Cycloveratrile Clathrates

The cycloveratrile clathrate compounds have been prepared by crystallization from a saturated solution of the host component as solute in the guest component as solvent[43].

The Tri-o-thymotide Clathrates

The preparation of these clathrate compounds is relatively simple. According to Lawton and Powell[156] most of the tri-o-thymotide clathrates may be crystallized from their solutions. They describe the preparation as follows:

"Usually tri-o-thymotide was dissolved in the other component which was heated to a suitable temperature. The solution on cooling deposited a crystalline adduct. In a few cases the nature of the product appeared to depend on the rate of cooling, a more ordered form of adduct resulting from the slower cooling. A few adducts were made by evaporation of solutions at room temperature. Sometimes the crystalline form which deposited was metastable and a second form gradually replaced it. When the other (guest) component was a solid it dissolved together with tri-o-thymotide in 2,2,4-trimethylpentane or 2,3-dimethylpentane, which do not form adducts. Cooling the solution caused the adduct to crystallize."

From Tables 3-5 and 3-6 in which the tri-*o*-thy-motide molecular compounds which they prepared are listed, it is obvious that the method has wide application.

The Cyclodextrin "Clathrates"

Though these compounds have not been definitely established as clathrate compounds, the question is still open to debate. The selectivity of their α-, β-, and γ- forms is interesting. When chlorine gas is passed through a solution of α-dextrin at $+10°C$, crystals of the inclusion compound precipitate. Bromine and iodine will form similar inclusion compounds. β-Dextrin will not form an inclusion compound with chlorine but will do so with bromine and iodine. γ-Dextrin will form an inclusion compound with

TABLE 4-1. INCLUSION COMPOUNDS OF α-CYCLODEXTRIN[71]

Gas	Moles of Gas per Moles of Cyclodextrin
Cl_2	0.3
Kr	0.34
Xe	0.85
O_2	0.32
CO_2	1.38
C_2H_4	0.64
CH_4	1.0
C_2H_6	1.0
C_3H_8	1.0
C_4H_{10}	1.2

iodine only[60]. Cramer and Henglein[71] have reported the preparation of the α-cyclodextrin inclusion compounds listed in Table 4-1. Lautsch and his associates[39,150—155] have included a comprehensive study of cyclodextrins with their work on inclusion compounds.

Clathrates of Inorganic Complexes

A series of compounds prepared by Hofmann and his co-workers[124,125,126] showed that a complex nickel-cyanide-ammonia compound could react with a small group of organic compounds to form additional compounds. When benzene is added to a solution of nickel cyanide in aqueous ammonia, a precipitate forms which has the composition, $Ni(CN)_2 \cdot NH_3 \cdot C_6H_6$. Thiophene, furan, pyrrole, aniline, and phenol react similarly with an ammoniacal solution of nickel cyanide. Powell and Rayner[225] have made a complete x-ray study of the structure of these compounds. The nature of the enclosure was not understood at the time of their original preparation. Double-salt clathrates of benzene have been prepared in which the Ni(II) of the cage structure has been replaced by Cu(II), Cd(II), or Zn(II)[28].

Hartley[118] prepared hexa(methyl*iso*cyanido)iron(II) chloride trihydrate, $Fe(CNCH_3)_6Cl_2 \cdot 3H_2O$, some fifty years ago. Powell and Bartindale[221] have delineated its clathrate structure by x-ray methods of analysis. Though they do not describe their method of preparation, they report having modified the original method. Hartley allowed methyl sulfate to react with dry potassium ferrocyanide, neutralized the product with a solution of barium hydroxide, treated it with barium chloride, filtered the resulting solution, and evaporated it under vacuum. Subsequent extraction with ethanol produced the complex compound which he called hexamethylferrocyanogen chloride. This compound will release two molecules of methyl chloride when heated to about 140°C for two to three hours under reduced pressure.

The preparation of clathrate compounds of inorganic complexes with many other organic molecules has been described by Schaeffer and co-workers[245] as "exceedingly simple." As a rule simple mixing of the solid complex with the organic component materials is all that is required. The reaction rates are usually very rapid—less than five minutes, and the clathrate crystals separate readily. The compounds listed in Table 2-4 are some of those which were used to form clathrates with xylenes, cymenes, methylnaphthalenes, and other organic molecules.

Since Schaeffer was studying the separation of mixtures his clathrates were formed selectively from "feed mixtures." Three principal methods were employed. They are: (1) stirring of the complex as a *suspension* in the liquid feed mixture, (2) contacting of the feed mixture with a solution of the clathrate former in a solvent at an elevated temperature, then cooling and filtering, and (3) contacting a suspension of the complex in an organic fluid (which does not dissolve the complex and which does not enter into the clathrating reaction) with the feed mixture. He observed that the best technique for a particular separation depended on the materials to be separated, the inorganic complex used, and the circumstances of manipulation.

The following two preparations are found in specific

examples of representative isomer separation techniques which were used by Schaeffer and co-workers:

Suspension Process. To a 150-ml beaker containing 20.0 gram (0.0365 mole) of tetra-(4-methylpyridino)-nickel dithiocyanate were added 55 ml of *n*-heptane and 3.0 ml of 4-methylpyridine. The resulting two-phase system was stirred by means of a stirring rod while 16.5 ml of 1:1 HCl and the hydrocarbon phase which separated was extracted into 30.0 ml of *n*-heptane. After separation of the liquid phase the hydrocarbon phase was washed twice with 30-ml portions of 1:1 HCl and then analyzed by means of ultraviolet spectroscopy. The analysis showed the *p*-xylene content in the xylenes present to be 57.2 per cent.

The remainder of the (clathrate) crystals on the filter were washed with 40 ml of *n*-heptane by reslurrying and refiltering. Acid decomposition of the washed crystals and ultraviolet examination of the xylene phase, as above, showed the *p*-xylene content in the xylenes present to be 68.3 per cent.

The combined filtrates were washed twice with 50-ml portions of 1:1 HCl and ultraviolet examination of the washed hydrocarbon phase showed the *p*-xylene content to be 4.3 per cent of the xylenes present.

Solution Process. To a 150-ml beaker containing 20.0 gram (0.0365 mole) of tetra-(4-methylpyridine)-nickel dithiocyanate was added 38.0 ml of methyl cellosolve and 4.0 ml of 4-methylpyridine. The mixture was heated on a hot plate to about 105° until solution was obtained. To the hot solution was added 16.5 ml (0.134 mole, 20.1 per cent *p*-xylene) of mixed xylene isomers;

then the solution was cooled in an ice-bath with continuous stirring. As the mixture cooled blue crystals of the clathrate compound separated. When cooled to about room temperature the mixture was filtered on a Büchner funnel. A 10.0-g aliquot of the crystals on the filter was dissolved in 60.0 ml of 1:1 HCl, and the hydrocarbon phase which separated was extracted into 30.0 ml of n-heptane. After separation of the liquid phases the hydrocarbon phase was washed twice with 30-ml portions of 1:1 HCl and then analyzed by means of ultraviolet spectroscopy. Analysis showed the p-xylene content in the xylenes present to be 61.8 per cent.

The remainder of the crystals on the filter were washed with 40.0 ml of methyl cellosolve by reslurrying and refiltering. Acid decomposition of the washed crystals and ultraviolet examination of the xylene phase, as above, showed the p-xylene content in the xylenes present to be 70.2 per cent.

The combined filtrates were diluted with 50 ml of n-heptane and washed three times with 40.0-ml portions of dilute HCl. Ultraviolet examination of the washed hydrocarbon phase showed the p-xylene content in xylenes present to be 3.7 per cent.

Hart and Smith[117] prepared the clathrate compound ot tetra-(methylpyridine)-nickel dithiocyanate with p-xylene. The inorganic complex was first formed by precipitation from a very dilute aqueous solution of nickel(II) chloride and 4-picoline to which an aqueous solution of potassium thiocyanate had been added. The complex was then suspended in a solution of

p-xylene in n-heptane from which the clathrate compound precipitated.

The preparations of the complexes and the clathrate compounds of Radzitsky and Hanotier[229], like those of Schaeffer *et. al.*, follow a uniform pattern. One example will suffice to illustrate the general procedure. Of the several methods which apply to the formation of clathrate compounds, and to the recovery of the clathrate, Radzitsky chose that of the titration of nickel thiocyanate with an amine in the presence of the compound to be enclathrated. The enclathrated compound could then be recovered by decomposition of the cage structure with a mineral acid. The following specific preparation of his clathrate compound of xylene with $Ni(SCN)_2$ (α-butylbenzylamine)$_4$ will illustrate his method:

A solution of 0.04 mole of $Ni(SCN)_2$ was prepared by dissolving 0.04 mole of $NiCl_2 \cdot 6\ H_2O$ and 0.08 mole of KSCN in 40 ml of water. To this solution, which was cooled in an ice bath, 0.18 mole of α-butylbenzylamine in xylene was added, with stirring. On addition of the amine a greenish-blue precipitate was formed. It gradually turned to a light blue color. After stirring for twenty minutes the precipitate—the xylene clathrate compound—was separated by filtration, washed twice with 100 ml samples of cold heptane and dried under vacuum for one hour at room temperature.

Baker and co-workers[15,16] described the preparation of many addition compounds of Dianin's compound. With liquid guest components the unsolvated Dianin's compound crystallized from the liquid component as solvent. In the case of methyl iodide, in which the compound is sparingly soluble, the unsolvated compound was placed in a Soxhlet apparatus thimble and extracted with methyl iodide. As the solvent became saturated, the clathrate compound separated.

The iodine-Dianin's compound clathrate was prepared by using decalin as the solvent. Although decalin also forms a clathrate compound with Dianin's compound, preferentially iodine will fill the available spaces. Ammonia and sulfur dioxide form clathrate compounds with Dianin's compound when it is allowed to dissolve in liquid NH_3 or SO_2 until the solution is saturated. The clathrate compound crystals separate slowly from the saturated solution. Piperidine forms a clathrate compound with Dianin's compound. The clathrate crystals separate from a saturated solution of Dianin's compound in piperidine. Many of the compounds which form clathrates with Dianin's compound are listed in Table 4-2.

Barrer[22] has shown that potassium benzenesulfonate forms nonstoichiometric, but reproducible, adducts with large molecules such as benzene and naphthalene whose composition is a function of temperature only. The compounds will form when the $KO_3SC_6H_5$ crystals are bathed in the hydrocarbon vapors under pressure.

The Novolak (2,2'-dihydroxy-5,5'-dimethyldiphenylmethane) *Tetramer Clathrate*

An interesting tetracyclic polymer addition compound, which may or may not be a true clathrate,

Table 4-2. Crystalline Adducts Formed by Dianin's
Compound[16]

Component	Mole Ratio* *Organic Compounds*
Methanol	2:1
Ethanol	3:1
Propan-2-ol	3:1
n-Butanol	3:1
tert.-Butanol	3:1
Acetone	3:1
Carbon tetrachloride	3:1
Methylene chloride	3:1
Methyl iodide	3:1
Nitromethane	3:1
Formic acid	3:1
Acetic acid	3:1
Propionic acid	4:1
Chloroform	4:1
Carbon disulfide	4:1
n-Butyric acid	5:1
n-Pentanol	6:1
n-Heptanol	6:1
Diethyl ether	6:1
1:3-Dibromopropane	6:1
Ethylene dichloride	6:1
Ethylene dibromide	6:1
Tetrachloroethylene	6:1
n-Butyl bromide	6:1
Diacetyl	6:1
Valeric acid	6:1
Hexanoic acid	6:1
Diethylamine	6:1
Ethyl chloroacetate	6:1
Benzene	6:1
Toluene	6:1
o-Xylene	6:1

* Mole ratio, Dianin's compound:component.

TABLE 4-2. CRYSTALLINE ADDUCTS FORMED BY DIANIN'S
COMPOUND[16] (*Continued*)

Component	Mole Ratio*
	Organic Compounds
m-Xylene	6:1
p-Xylene	6:1
Bromobenzene	6:1
Iodobenzene	6:1
o-Dichlorobenzene	6:1
Diisobutylene	7:1
tert.-Pentyl alcohol	7:1
Ethyl acetate	7:1
Isopentyl valerate	7:1
p-Bromoanisole	7:1
m-Dichlorobenzene	7:1
2-Bromopyridine	7:1
2:6-Lutidine	7:1
3-Methylheptane (tech.)	8:1
1-Methylnaphthalene	8:1
Pyridine	8:1
Triethylamine	9:1
"Decalin"	9:1
"Decalin"	17:1
	Inorganic Compounds
Sulfur dioxide	4:1
Ammonia	6:1
Iodine	7:1

was prepared by the condensation of 2,2'-dihydroxy-5,5'-dimethyl-3,3'-bis-hydroxymethyldiphenylmethane with an excess of p-cresol[130]. A mixture of the dialcohol (10 g), p-cresol (88 g), and concentrated HCl (8 ml) was heated on a water bath for two hours, distilled in steam to remove the excess cresol and dissolved in benzene (200 ml). The crude polymer (9.7 g; melting point 172 to 178°C) was precipitated with light petroleum. On recrystallization from ethylene dichloride the addition complex was obtained as hexagonal plates. It was found to be a stable 1:1 addition compound and believed to be a clathrate.

Evidently structural studies on molecular compounds lag far behind other studies concerning their nature. Where simple sterically caused inclusion is suspected, quite often it has not been confirmed. It probably occurs far more frequently than has been indicated. A striking example of this may be seen in the work of Baker, et al.[15], who reported the formation of 1:1 molecular complexes with 2'-hydroxy-2,4,4,7,4'-pentamethyflavan and many ethers, ketones, and amines. These guest molecules are listed in Table 4-3. Although salt formation may and undoubtedly does play some part in the formation of some of these complexes, the size and structure of the combining molecules are of importance, particularly with ethers and ketones.

The general method for their preparation is as follows: The flavan (2 g) is dissolved in light petroleum (boiling point 40 to 60°C) and the other component (ca. 1 g) is added. In many cases the complexes begin to separate almost immediately; furthermore if the mixture is stirred, the separation of fine crystals is complete in a few minutes. Large crystals form quite commonly if the mixture is not disturbed. In a few cases crystallization may require a minimum of a day.

The 2-iodopyridine complex with the flavan appears similar to hydroquinone-formic acid and to hydroquinone-acetylene clathrate compounds. Also, it is com-

TABLE 4-3. CRYSTALLINE COMPLEXES FORMED BY
2'-Hydroxy-2:4:4:7:4'-Pentamethylflavan[15]

Component in 1:1 Complexes

Diethyl ether
Di*iso*propyl ether
Diethylketone
Di*iso*propyl ketone
Methyl *n*-propyl ketone
Mesityl oxide
Acetylacetone
Diethylamine
Diethylmethylamine
Triethylamine
Di-*n*-propylamine
Di*iso*propylamine
Di-*n*-butylamine
Di-*sec*-butylamine
Cyclohexylamine
Benzylamine
Aniline
Pyridine
N-Ethylpiperidine
2-Methylpyridine
3-Methylpyridine
4-Methylpyridine
2:4-Dimethylpyridine
2:6-Dimethylpyridine
Quinoline
*Iso*quinoline
2-Methyl quinoline
2-Bromopyridine
3-Bromopyridine
2-Iodopyridine
2-Chloroquinoline
(-)-Coniine

Component in other complexes, $C_{20}H_{24}O_2:H_2O:Component = 2:2:1.$

Dioxan
Morpholine

pletely stable on exposure to light, whereas 2-iodo-pyridine usually becomes brown on exposure to light over a period of time. Apparently the molecule enclosed in the lattice is completely protected from oxidation. Such observations lead one strongly to suspect clathrate formation.

As these preparations have shown, the formation of clathrate compounds is usually a straightforward crystallization of the adduct from solutions which require only conditions which normally are encountered in laboratory procedures. The very low temperature and high pressure conditions for the gas clathrate formations are the exception; evidently clathrate compounds have often been prepared by many an unsuspecting chemist.

CHAPTER 5

Use of Clathrate Compounds

It has been shown that clathrate compounds, cage-like inclusion compounds, result from a more specialized selectivity than is found in the case of either channel or layer inclusion compounds. Although their identification as a separate group is relatively recent, with the swift advance of the study of the urea inclusion compounds a pathway has been cut through the unfamiliar jungle of inclusion compounds— compounds that have been with us a long time, but whose existence and potential we have been slow to recognize. The immediate application of Bengen's work, followed by the extension of it which has advanced at a steady pace, has served to open up a number of new avenues of research. Concomitant applications, both laboratory and industrial, are inevitable.

The application of spatial "fitting together" of molecules has already proved to be amazingly effective in the laboratory in effecting separations which were hitherto difficult. Other uses as well have been found, and all types of inclusion compounds, layer, channel, and cage have been employed. With Bengen's[29] discovery of urea's channel inclusion of aliphatic straight-chain molecules, which could be used as a means of separation of hydrocarbons, numerous investigations began. These have produced an ever-lengthening list of compounds whose inclusion properties have been demonstrated.

At an even earlier date the peculiar behavior of choleic acids was observed by Wieland and Sorge[310] and studies by Go and Kratky[112] later showed the choleic acid complexes to be composed of large desoxycholic acid structures in which there were channels which enclosed such aliphatic monobasic fatty acids as palmitic, stearic, and oleic. More recently it has been shown that each individual choleic acid complex has a higher melting point than either of its components. Other fatty acids such as butyric acid, and certain aromatic compounds such as phenol, benzaldehyde, camphor, and naphthalene were found also to complex with desoxycholic acid. Since this preliminary work certain other steroids have been reported to be capable of forming addition compounds. Both cortisone and cholic acid form blue-iodine channel type complexes with iodine, and digitonin forms highly specific complexes with other steroids[313]. In a biochemistry review article Sobotka[276] discussed, "... the stubborn tenacity by which fatty acids are retained whenever the purification of bile acids has been attempted."

To stimulate interest in the potential uses for clathrate compounds and for the clathration process it has

seemed advisable to refer to some of the urea and thiourea inclusion studies, along with those of the clathrate compounds. It is highly probable that many of
these urea investigations have their counterpart in
the clathrate field and need only to be elucidated.
Indeed, there must be times when cage inclusion is
favored over channel or layer inclusion, and vice versa.

As their structures suggest, clathrate compounds
have specific characteristics which may be applied in
the separation, identification, or analysis of certain
compounds. Particularly in cases in which the physical properties of two or more compounds are not
sufficiently different to permit their use to effect separation, there may be markedly different geometrical
forms. Isomers exemplify this situation. Even ordinary standard methods of fractionation may fail to
separate compounds having similar physical properties. The urea addition compounds selectively separate straight chain hydrocarbons from those having
branched chains; nevertheless a separation by chain
length does not necessarily follow. In clathrate compounds the restricted cage measurements permit a
greater refinement of the selectivity process.

Evans and his associates[87] purified benzene from its
usual contaminants by means of clathration. They
began with a moderately pure grade of benzene. Although thiophene and benzene both form monoam-
minenickel(II) cyanide complexes, benzene appears
more firmly held in the cage structure; consequently
it is preferentially enclathrated[76]. By crystallization
of the complex, monoamminenickel(II) cyanide, the

benzene clathrate is formed from impure benzene. After it is removed from the solution, the pure benzene can be readily recovered. Jones and Fay[134] also used the same basic technique to recover benzene from hydrocarbon mixtures. Benzene-C^{14} has been prepared from neutron irradiation of this monoamminenickel-(II) cyanide-benzene clathrate[315].

Separations of the rare gases have been most effectively carried out by selective clathration. Argon may be separated from neon by adjustment of the pressure conditions to those under which argon forms a hydroquinone-argon clathrate; however neon does not. Krypton may be separated from xenon by taking advantage of the greater solubility of xenon. Powell and his co-workers[38] have made a thorough study of these separations.

The use of inclusion compounds to bring about the resolution of *racemic* mixtures is a new and promising method of resolution. Urea was used by Schlenk[32, 262] with aliphatic molecules. Secondary octyl chloride and other substances were separated into enantiomorphous forms.

In the case of clathrate compounds molecular shapes are even more crucial in the inclusion process. *Dextro-* and *levo-* molecules may be separated. When the host structure consists of an arrangement of atoms which is not superimposable on its mirror-image, the cavities also will be different from their mirror-images; consequently they may be able to include one form of a guest molecule while rejecting its enantiomorph. Dissymmetry of an enclosing structure may arise when the cage-forming material is optically active, optically inactive, or *racemic*.

Cyclodextrin inclusion compounds are examples of those in which the host structure is itself optically active. A partial resolution of such compounds as mandelic ester has been made with cyclodextrin. Cramer[65] first reported the partial resolution of the

TABLE 5-1. RESOLUTION WITH β-CYCLODEXTRIN[68]

Compound	Rotation $[\alpha]_D{}^{25}$	Per Cent Resolution
dl-$C_6H_5CHBrCO_2Et$	$-$ 0.92° (EtOH)	5.75
dl-$C_6H_5CHOHCO_2Et$	$-$ 5.90° (CS$_2$)	3.32
dl-Ethyl atrolacetate	$-$ 2.23° (EtOH)	8.35
dl-o-ClC$_6$H$_4$CHOHCO$_2$Et	$-$12.65° (EtOH)	—
dl-Menthyl acetate	$-$ 1.42° (MeOH)	1.78
dl-Menthyl chloroacetate	$-$ 1.72° (MeOH)	2.21
dl-p-ClC$_6$H$_4$CHOHCOC$_6$H$_4$Cl-p	$+$ 4.62° (EtOAc)	—
dl-o-ClC$_6$H$_4$CHOHCOC$_6$H$_4$Cl-o	$+$ 1.50° (EtOAc)	—
dl-$C_6H_5CHOMeOCC_6H_5$	$+$ 0.79° (EtOH)	0.84
dl-$C_6H_5CHBrCO_2H$	$+$ 7.71° (EtOH)	11.33
dl-Menthol	$-$ 2.44° (EtOH)	4.88
dl-α,α'-dibromosuccinic acid	$+$12.10° (EtOH)	8.18
dl-Atrolactic acid	$-$ 2.90° (H$_2$O)	5.57
dl-Ethyl phenylchloroacetate	$-$ 3.40° (EtOH)	3.15

ethyl esters of mandelic acid, phenylchloroacetic acid, and phenylbromoacetic acid. The resulting resolutions ranged from 0.5 to 16 per cent. An extension of this work, using β-cyclodextrin and a number of other esters, Table 5-1, appeared in the literature some years later[68]; however the maximum resolution obtained was about 12 per cent.

When a structure, for example a cage structure, is

composed of optically active molecules of a substance which is used as a racemate it may form a non-enantiomorphous cage structure composed of equal numbers of *d*- and *l*-molecules. The product may be a structure composed of cavities which will not be dissymmetric, or they may occur in mirror-image pairs like the enclosing molecules. Selectivity of *d*- or *l*-guest molecules will not occur when such a structure crystallizes to form a clathrate.

Newman and Powell[177] reported the spontaneous resolution of solvated tri-*o*-thymotide. Newman explained[176] and illustrated the steric factors involved. The crystallization of tri-*o*-thymotide from benzene produced host molecules of tri-*o*-thymotide in the crystal structure which belongs to only one of the enantiomorphous space groups—that possessing a screw axis of symmetry. In this manner the separation of the two enantiomorphous forms of the thymotide crystals was achieved. Although this resolution has been accomplished, the product racemizes very rapidly, having a half-life period of a few minutes at room temperature.

Lawton and Powell[156] greatly extended this work and reported at least fifty complexes with tri-*o*-thymotide in which spontaneous optical resolution occurred. In general, the tri-*o*-thymotide was dissolved in the guest component and heated to a suitable temperature. The rate of cooling was controlled to give optimum formation. When the tri-*o*-thymotide is crystallized from a solvent which is itself a *racemic* mixture and forms with it a molecular compound, the cavities of any one crystal will enclose preferentially the *dextro-* or *levo-* form of solvent molecule. Any process for separating the two different tri-*o*-thymotide crystals should simultaneously separate the solvent optical isomers.

The size of the molecules to be resolved should be the only limiting factor in this method of resolution. Its chief advantage lies in the fact that no chemical reactions occur and no change of configuration is possible. Because the shape of the molecule is the only basis on which enclathration is determined, no reactive group is needed. The observation of the large initial rotations of tri-*o*-thymotide provides a method of sorting small quantities of materials, quantities too small to show their own rotation. Still smaller amounts may be handled in mixtures with carrier solvents. When both carrier and solute form complexes, sorting should resolve the rare constituent occupying only a few cavities. When, in exceptional cases, the solvent is either the *dextro-* or *levo-* form, no sorting is necessary. From one known absolute configuration of a guest molecule in a tri-*o*-thymotide clathrate and a detailed structure determination, Powell believes it is possible that one could determine the absolute configuration of the cavities corresponding to each enantiomorphic crystalline form. Then the absolute configuration of other molecules could be deduced by observing the form of the tri-*o*-thymotide with which they combine by inclusion.

Dalgliesh[77] discussed the resolution of *racemic* mixtures by paper chromatography from the standpoint of adsorption and the structural features of the adsorbent. In their comprehensive work on chromatography Lederer and Lederer[157] report the type of inclusion and resolution of various *racemic* mixtures by such materials as modified ion exchange resin, starch, wool, casein, paper, and processed silica gel. None of these applications has been analyzed sufficiently to identify the specific type of inclusion involved, but it is commonly believed that inclusion is the basic process.

Kemula and Sybilska[137] have described in detail the successful application of partition and adsorption chromatography to the separation of mixtures of isomers, taking advantage of the size and shape selectivity for clathrate compound formation. Analysis by the chromato-polarographic method[138] was carried out in order to separate isomeric nitrophenols, nitroanilines, chloronitrobenzenes, and nitrotoluenes. In all cases a quantitative separation of the *ortho*-isomer from the other isomers was obtained. Separations of mixtures of nitroaliphatic compounds were also made, but with less ease. Their preliminary work was done with the clathrate-former tetra(4-methylpyridino)-nickel dithiocyanate prepared by the method of Schaeffer and co-workers[245]. Later they found it more satisfactory to prepare another complex by using, for precipitation, a mixture of β- and γ-picoline and 2,6-lutidine instead of pure γ-picoline. The *ortho*-isomers are found in the first fraction of eluate and can be very accurately determined polarographically. By using more concentrated solutions of potassium thiocyanate, *meta*- and *para*- isomers can be eluated. They report that in some instances the mobile phase composition can be so chosen that it is possible to separate completely all three isomers in one process.

Krebs and co-workers[147,148] have patented methods for the resolution of dl-phenylglycine, N-benzoyl-dl-alanine, dl-valine, dl-phenylalanine, dl-asparaginic acid dl-serine, dl-cysteine, and the N-acetyl and N-formyl derivatives of dl-isoleucine. Their method is based on the adsorption of the isomers on starch columns; however the specific nature of the inclusion has not been reported.

The research carried out by workers in the petroleum industries has been a potent source of stimulation of interest in clathrate compounds. Possibly the greatest strides to date have been made in the separations of petroleum fractions[4,5,8]. Other applications have been of a more academic nature; however there are signs of an awakening of interest in the field of nuclear chemistry and in certain large-scale industrial purification processes.

Shortly after Bengen's work became known, both Schlenk[260] and Smith[270,271,272] clarified the structure of the paraffin-urea compounds. The application of unusual properties of paraffin-urea complexes followed shortly. Approximately a year later Angla[2,3] prepared the thiourea complexes which Schlenk[261] showed to be very similar to those of urea, differing mainly in the diameter of the inclusion channel. The specificity of urea[34,35,302] and thiourea adducts for distinguishing between unbranched and branched chain molecules, respectively, was one of the first properties of these compounds to be utilized. The application of this specificity was made in the method of separation known as "Extractive Crystallization."

A comprehensive review of work on inclusion compounds, especially those of urea and thiourea, by Kobe and Domask[145] appeared in 1952. Special emphasis was placed on the use of these compounds in the extractive crystallization method for the separation of hydrocarbons[115,32,136,159,160,295,306,162]. Undoubtedly many of the methods which were reported at that time for the use of urea and thiourea can, with suitable modifications, be applied to analogous compounds which form clathrates. The rapid development of the extractive crystallization method may be said to have set the pattern for the use of countless other inclusion compounds. Bengen's work which was carried on in Germany, was kept secret until after World War II. Initially it appeared on a microfilm prepared by Technical Oil Mission, which made the information available to industry[30]. Bailey, Smith, and others[13,14,234,235,236] have greatly extended Bengen's work.

In his review, Kobe assumed that the initial applications of extractive crystallization would be restricted to the separation of close boiling isomers and to special refining and separation problems. However, Fetterly[95] suggested a number of other possibilities; for example, subjecting feed streams from certain petroleum refining operations to extractive crystallization to remove either naphthenes, or paraffins, in order to cut down by-products.

Once the versatility of the method became known

many other applications were suggested. Medicinals, household sprays, and many hydrocarbons utilized for chemical purposes are frequently required to be colorless. The purification of these compounds by extractive crystallization appears to offer the possibility of an inexpensive and satisfactory process for their preparation. Also, it was recognized that a clathrate as a crystalline carrier for certain hydrocarbons in which fumigants dissolve would be decidedly advantageous. Inclusion of the hydrocarbon and/or the fumigant in a clathrate compound, where the material is enclosed in a solid and where its release can be simply controlled, offers possibilities to manufacturers of certain types of products.

The inclusion of fatty acids in urea and in thiourea has been proposed as a method of protecting the acids from oxidation over a period of time; for example, linoleic acid is unaltered after having stood in its urea adduct form and exposed to air for one month[259,269]. From their studies along these lines Schlenk and coworkers[255,256,257,258] suggested inclusion as a general method of protecting certain molecules from air oxidation.

As a follow up of this study they and others investigated adducts of α-dextrin, β-dextrin, and deoxycholic acid with linoleic acid, linolenic acid, methyl linolenate, cinnamaldehyde, and vitamin A palmitate. All were found to be very resistant to auto-oxidation. Fieser and Newman[97] prepared desoxycholic acid-alkaloid adducts. Caglioti and associates[41,42] have studied the structures of some of these compounds, whereas

Clasen[53] investigated polymerization in channel inclusion compounds.

The use of urea-inclusion compounds of essential fatty acids was recommended by Holman and Ener[127] as a means of supplementation in the diet, by way of the ration, thereby affording protection to those unstable substances such as fatty acids and vitamin A.

Because of the inclusion of carbon tetrachloride with dry thiourea, it has been suggested that adduct formation may prove to be a method for the recovery of certain volatile solvents. This points to the possibilities of vast savings on the part of certain industries as well as to the removal of serious health or psychological problems which have arisen in local communities where volatile waste products have been potentially hazardous, or merely annoying.

A number of other unrelated but interesting uses have been proposed. The use of an α-dextrin clathrate of carbon dioxide as a baking powder has been patented[258]. The separation of inert gases on the basis of hydrate stability differences has been proposed[181]. The inclusion complexes of N-1-naphthylphthalamic acid with certain high molecular weight substances have been tested as herbicides[273]. Dry potato starch has been found effective for the separation of certain organic compounds because it takes up such compounds as carbon tetrachloride, methylene chloride, carbon disulfide, nitrobenzene, pyridine, and petroleum ether[296]. It is known that selective clathration is a satisfactory method for effecting the substitution of the ring hydrogen of metal β-dicarbonyl chelates with bromine, without any intermediate ring cleavage[144].

The analytical applications of inclusion compounds are in their infancy. The use of urea and thiourea inclusion compounds in analysis has been investigated to some small extent. Observing what has been done with them will lead to investigations along similar lines with the clathrates. Zimmerscheid, *et al.*[318] studied hydrocarbon analysis by inclusion compound formation. At the time of their first report they felt that further developments and modifications of the techniques were advised but that the method was potentially a useful one for the analysis of complex petroleum fractions. A review of the literature on the inclusion compounds of mixtures of organic acids, esters, etc., will provide ideas for many other organic compound mixture analyses.

A discussion of the separation of fatty acids and their derivatives by urea extractive crystallization was published by Newey, *et al.*[178]. According to the report, when fatty acids are mixed with a saturated aqueous or alcoholic solution of urea, or when they are ground with solid urea, crystalline inclusion compounds form with the saturated fraction of the acid mixture. When the inclusion compound fraction is filtered off, a raffinate of high iodine value remains. The urea inclusion compounds subsequently can be decomposed readily with an excess of water to recover the extracted fraction. The investigators also proposed other uses of the method which according to them is, " . . . simple, relatively inexpensive, and operates at room temperature." Although urea has the advantage over most of the known clathrating agents of being relatively inexpensive, it is very probable that in cases where clathrate formation is indicated over urea adduct formation the advantages will outweigh the cost.

The work of Zimmerscheid and his associates[319] on the separation of linear aliphatic compounds by inclusion with urea was among the earliest of its kind. The n-alkanes and their linear derivatives were shown to form inclusion compounds with urea, whereas most branched and cyclic hydrocarbons and their derivatives did not. It was evident from this work that in the authors' words, "The technique has a multitude of research applications in the separation of mixtures, in the purification and identification of compounds, and as a means of analysis." The interpretation which was given in their report includes a summary of urea inclusion and its place among, and resemblance to, the various types of compounds which exhibit inclusion properties. The possibility of the use of other types of inclusion compounds in similar work was implied.

From the time of the report on the laboratory investigations of Zimmerscheid to that of Bailey and co-workers[14] a time lapse of little more than one year occurred. The latter report was of a pilot plant process, of two barrels a day capacity, which had proved conclusively that a continuous operation of hydrocarbon separations on a commercial basis would be practical.

In a study of fast fundamental transfer processes in aqueous biomolecular systems the biologists have been examining hydrates by electron microscopy and electron diffraction. They propose the use of hydrates as a basis for direct studies of biological systems in their native hydrated state. Noting that the open structure of water favors clathrate formation, Fernández-Morán[93] has reported investigations to visualize directly the water structure in cell constituents by local formation of xenon and argon hydrates and moiré imaging through superimposed isomorphic crystals. Through combined studies of this type biologists hope to gain a better understanding of the fine structure of living biological systems which are unquestionably linked at the molecular level with their essential water component.

Cramer[63], Gottschalk[116], and others[150,153,167,184] have discussed the mode of enzyme action, assuming an inclusion of the substrate by the enzyme molecule. Cramer has called attention to the cyclodextrins as compounds useful in differentiating, by means of inclusion, between isomeric forms. These observations revive, extend, and provide a new approach to the old "lock-and-key" theory of enzymes.

The inclusion of certain compounds alters their oxidation-reduction potentials. Methylene blue has a potential of -0.027 v (pH $= 8.3$) which is elevated to $+0.021$ v (pH $= 8.3$) on addition of cyclodextrin. The catalytic action of inclusion compounds has been reported by Weiss and Hofmann[308], by Barrer[24], and by Cramer[62]. It is illustrated by the oxidation of diphenylamine in its included form. Also, cyclodextrins are capable of catalyzing the oxidation of certain α-hydroxyketones via the corresponding enediols.

Eley[86] has reviewed the electrical conductivity of crystalline organic substances. Organic semiconductors may be either pure organic compounds or molecular complexes, especially crystalline solids, which show a specific conductance which increases with temperature. He refers to studies[10,44,166] which indicated the possible importance of this semi-conductivity in biological problems, for example, chlorophyll-protein complexes in photosynthesis and carcinogenic hydrocarbon-protein complexes.

There are strong factors favoring the listing of the haptens among the biologically important inclusion compounds. Hapten is the term introduced for the nonproteinoid portion of an antigen that determines the specificity of antigen to antibody. Polysaccharides, as well as certain other chemical substances, can act as haptens, and their nature has been reviewed by Campbell and Bulman[45]. The antigen and antibody are bound mainly by very weak Van der Waals' forces. Cramer comments that these do not lead to fixation of molecules; however, in the case of close "fitting-in," the combined weak bond forces result in one strong bond.

Again, whether or not proteins form inclusion compounds, and if so, to what extent and what type is of great interest to biologists. It is not yet known whether such compounds as dye-stuff complexes of serum albumin[48,120,142,143], chromoproteins, like ovoverdin[149], or even hemoglobin[192,193,152] may be formulated as inclusion compounds; nevertheless the possibility has not been excluded[58]. Cramer sees reasons both for and against believing them to be types of inclusion compounds[59]. He says that the specificity of their reactions points to inclusion, and normal salt formation may exclude it. The decision must await further studies in the field.

Many macromolecules are helixes in which the molecules of one component are wound around those of a second component. Only recently has there been a major breakthrough to some understanding of the nature of their structures. The molecular structure of deoxyribonucleic acid has been shown to resemble an inclusion compound. According to Feughelman[96] and others[83] the nucleic acid helix has a groove running through the macromolecule in a screw-line. The consensus of opinion seems to be that protamines combine with nucleic acid by fitting into this "ditch" and that the biological activity of nucleic acids is related in some way to this unusual structure. Fresco and Alberts[101,102] have made some interesting observations on the structure of deoxyribonucleic acid (DNA) and the probable way that gene mutations fit into the molecules.

No attempt will be made here to discuss the tremendous amount of work which has been, and is currently, in progress on these biologically strategic molecules[33]. Perutz[194] summarized the importance of their study and the elucidation of their relationship to the molecular basis of life. After examining an electron micro-photograph of chromosomes one investigator is reported to have said that the picture showed, " . . . a hierarchy of pairs of pairs of pairs of strands."

It would be hard to imagine an area in which there are more avenues for investigation than that of the structures of molecules in biological systems. Even the degree of inclusion, whether in part, as in channel inclusion, or *in toto*, as in clathrates, or by some type of bonding, may prove to be the key to the ultimate understanding of their activities.

Fuller[108] has described a two-stranded helical configuration for ribonucleic acid which is similar to the DNA B configuration. "Double stranded helical regions can be formed either by intermolecular hydrogen bonding between the two RNA strands or by intra-molecular hydrogen bonding between different parts of a single stranded model of RNA proposed by Fresco, *et al.*[102,103]. Franklin and associates, among others, have discussed the structure of RNA[99].

One of the most ingenious uses to which clathrate compounds have been put, and one likely to be widely adopted or extended, is that of Chleck and Ziegler[49,50,128]. They devised a new way of handling radioactive krypton, Kr^{85}, to provide a safe and useful source of *beta* radiation. Krypton's chemical inertness and its failure to enter into a metabolic process makes it particularly advantageous from the biological standpoint. By enclathrating it in a hydroquinone cage it becomes relatively easy to handle. As the crystalline hydroquinone krypton clathrate the *beta* source can be powdered into small crystal dimensions with little loss of radioactivity. Much greater ease of handling results.

The authors claim the hydroquinone-Kr^{85} clathrate

to be among the safest forms of radioactivity. The Kr^{85} is virtually a pure *beta* emitter and does not require heavy shielding for safe handling. If the radioactive atoms are released from their cage, they are rapidly diluted and carried away by the atmosphere. If the gas is accidentally inhaled, it is incapable of being either absorbed or metabolized by the body. Finally, its decay product is not radioactive so only the original krypton has any hazard potential.

Some of the uses to which the hydroquinone-Kr^{85} clathrate can be put are described in the study in which the authors report that they are continuing their investigations. At the time of publication they had in operation an experimental air-pollution monitor which operates on the principle that if the material to be detected can oxidize the clathrate cage, and thereby destroy it, the released Kr^{85} can be measured by means of the conventional radiation detectors. The hydroquinone-Kr^{85} clathrate is sensitive to sulfur dioxide, ozone, chlorine dioxide, and other contaminants in the parts-per-billion range.

Speed, ease, low cost, and portability of the simple and rugged instruments were cited as advantages of this detection method. The hydroquinone-krypton clathrate may also be applied: (1) to the gauging of thickness, (2) as an x-ray source when mixed with one or more elements that emit the desired energy, (3) for static elimination, and (4) to provide a light source by combination with a scintillator such as zinc sulfide.

Following the successful separations of aliphatic

compounds which were induced by their selective inclusion with urea and thiourea and the application of these separations in the petroleum industry, Schaeffer and Dorsey announced a new separation. Their process was described in a science news journal as "Union Oil's New Clathration Process[4]." As the name indicated, clathration was the basis for the process which was recognized as potentially very valuable and almost limitless in its application. The first report was made at the 132nd meeting of the American Chemical Society at which the work was described before the Division of Industrial and Engineering Chemistry. The recovery of p-xylene from either C_8 aromatic hydrocarbons or gasolines by single-step operations was described as possible by means of preferential clathration, when the proper complex and manipulative conditions were chosen. It is of significance that the investigators foresaw the possibilities of the method. The abstract of their paper reads in part as follows:

Industrial potentialities for this method may arise in many fields: production of p-xylene or p-cymene for terephthalic acid manufacture, production of m-xylene for isophthalic acid manufacture; recovery of chemicals from coal tar, coal hydrogenation products, petroleum, or shale oil; manipulation of natural products or pharmaceutical intermediates; analytical segregation of fractions of complex mixtures.

In Chapter 4 the methods and techniques which

were employed by Schaeffer and his co-workers for the preparation of the clathrate compounds from petroleum mixtures were described. Following the preparations the methods for the recovery of the desired component from a clathrate were given by Schaeffer, and they constitute the important practical phase of the process[245]. Any one of the three procedures may be employed.

The first of these procedures was a simple dissolving of the clathrate compound in an aqueous acid solution. Frequently the cage structure is destroyed in this manner so that when the guest molecules are not notably soluble in the acid solution they can be separated and recovered readily.

Steam stripping of the clathrate framework is the second suggested procedure. Schaeffer and his co-workers tested this method on the removal of xylenes from their tetra-(4-methylpyridino)-nickel dithiocyanato cages and found not only were relatively large amounts of steam required, but also that hydrocarbon recovery was not complete. An attempt to draw xylene from its complex cage by the application of a vacuum required a pressure-temperature combination at which both the clathrate compound and the molecular compound (the cage) dissociated. The third method, which was generally most successful, employed the high solubility-temperature coefficients of some of the complexes in various solvents. The procedure required the clathrate compound to be suspended in the solvent; then the mixture was heated until it dissolved. The complexes employed showed no solubility in organic solvents; consequently the liberated guest molecules may be removed by either distillation or liquid-liquid extraction. The effectiveness of this process is illustrated by the results given in Tables 3-17, 3-18 and 3-20, where some of the data for separation of p-xylene are given.

The hydrocarbon hydrate method[79,80,107,131,294] which has been developed recently has been applied to the conversion of saline water to fresh water[6]. The hydrate-hydrocarbon clathrate crystals which are formed may be separated from the brine and washed. At a temperature of 45°F and a pressure of 70 psig they yield potable water. It is estimated that this method will produce fresh water at less than fifty cents per one thousand gallons in a ten million gallon-a-day plant. Plans for pilot plant testing the method were underway at the time of the report. One advantage of this use of clathration is that the process takes less energy than regular freezing processes because the crystals form above the freezing point temperature of water.

The uses given in this chapter for molecular compounds, varied and wide ranging as they are, illustrate the versatility of inclusion compounds and the inclusion process, of clathrate compounds and of clathration. Specific details of each application are available in nearly all of the references cited. In particular, the work of Schaeffer and his associates is described mainly in the patent literature.

CHAPTER 6

Prospectus of Clathrate Compounds

The enthusiasm with which any work on the application of clathrate compounds or the use of the clathration process has been greeted argues well for the future of clathrates. The field of inclusion compounds *per se* is young, and that of clathrate compounds is in its infancy. In some cases the startling results of research ventures seem almost fortuitous. Attention has been called to the fact that one book[58] and at least 18 review articles* on various aspects of the subject of inclusion chemistry have appeared within the past twelve years[119].

It has been said that the clathration process may solve problems which have held back coal hydrogenation's growth for many years[4]. Also, clathration may clarify the problems encountered in other separation processes such as those common to shale oil streams, coal tar distillates, and other petroleum streams. Pharmaceutical preparations by clathration separations appear promising. The clathrating technique is

*Starred references in Bibliography.

seen as having, in certain applications, definite economic and quality advantages over other methods of purifying hard-to-separate isomers.

Of the more recent reports, there is one in which more than eight hundred clathrations, using thirty-four different inorganic (Werner) complexes, were studied[228]. Clathration not only offers a technique for the separation of aromatic isomers, but also is believed to facilitate the way for the separation of compounds from petroleum aromatic extracts. Economically the separation of many of these compounds has been considered out of the question in the past.

In the field of organic synthesis the cost of pharmaceuticals and of high purity photographic chemicals may feasibly be significantly diminished by syntheses which produce isomer mixtures separable by clathration.

The gas analysis studies of Ziegler and his associates have opened the area of clathrate compound applications to analysis for ammonia, phosphorus and arsenic compounds, sulfur dioxide, hydrocarbons, and water vapor. They suggest its application to air pollution studies, process control, meteorology, and "many other fields, limited only by the imagination." They believe the technique to be applicable to a wide range of materials.

The resolutions of *racemic* mixtures which have been effected are in the early stages of investigation. Under the proper conditions, it is anticipated that 100 per cent resolution should be possible. The basic research on the nature of both the clathrate compounds themselves and on the mechanism of the clathration process is underway but far from complete. With each new clarification will come greater and more diversified adaptations and applications.

The studies on hydrate clathrates lead to speculations which approach the realm of fantasy. Kingery[140] recently discussed the need for "alloying" ice and snow in order to improve their qualities as structural materials. The United States Army is interested in excavating tunnels and constructing chambers in glacial ice and snow in arctic regions. Is clathration the answer? Pauling[191a] reported studies which indicate that anesthesia may be attributed to the formation in the brain of minute hydrate crystals of the clathrate type.

In view of the possibilities of predesigning a clathrating agent from our knowledge of the hundreds, probably thousands, which have been prepared or proposed, it becomes immediately apparent that the field of selective clathration stretches limitlessly ahead. A literature search covering investigations on clathrate compounds over the past decade and a half reveals a steady growth in interest in these unusual compounds. The work of Powell has set into motion a whole new field of investigation which does not lack direction though, at present, it lacks order.

References

1. Andrew, E. R., *J. Phys. Chem. Solids*, **18**, 9 (1961).
2. Angla, B., *Ann. chim.*, **4**, (12), 639 (1949).
3. Angla, B., *Compt. rend.*, **224**, 402, 1166 (1947).
4. Anon., *Chem. Eng. News*, **35**, (38), 78 (1957).
5. Anon., *Chem. Eng. News*, **36**, (2), 43 (1958).
6. Anon., *Chem. Eng. News*, **39**, (1), 37 (1961).
7. Anon., *Chem. Eng. News*, **39**, (7), 40 (1961).
8. Anon., *Chem. Eng. News*, **39**, (15), 47 (1961).
9. Arcos, J. C., and Arcos, M., *Naturwiss.*, **42**, 651 (1955); *C.A.* **52**, 3105c (1958).
10. Arnold, W., and Sherwood, H. K., *Proc. Natl. Acad. Sci. U.S.*, **43**, 105 (1957).
11. Aynsley, E. E., Campbell, W. A., and Dodd, R. E., *Proc. Chem. Soc.*, **1957**, 210.
12. Badger, G. M., "The Structures and Reactions of the Aromatic Compounds," p. 86, Cambridge, University Press, 1954.
13. Bailey, W. A., Jr., Bannerot, B. A., Fetterly, L. C., Gable, C. M., Millard, R. W., Redlich, O., and Smith, A. E., "Proc. 3rd World Petrol. Congr., Hague, 1951," Section III, p. 161.
14. Bailey, W. A., Jr., Bannerot, B. A., Fetterly, L. C., and Smith, A. E., *Ind. Eng. Chem.*, **43**, 2125 (1951).
15. Baker, W., Curtis, R. F., and Edwards, M. G., *J. Chem. Soc.*, **1951**, 83.
16. Baker, W., Floyd, A. J., McOmie, J. F. W., Pope, G., Weaving, A. S., and Wild, J. H., *J. Chem. Soc.*, **1956**, 2010, 2018.
17. Baker, W., and McOmie, J. F. W., *Chemistry & Industry (London)*, **1955**, 256.

18. Barlow, G. B., and Clamp, A. C., *J. Chem. Soc.*, **1961**, 393.

*19. Barnett, E. de B., and Wilson, C. L., "Inorganic Chemistry," 2nd ed., New York, Longmans, Green & Company, 1957.

20. Baron, Maximo, *Org. Chem. Bull.*, **29**, (2), 1 (1957); (3), 1 (1957).

21. Barrer, R. M., *Quart. Revs. (London)*, **3**, 293 (1949).

22. Barrer, R. M., *Nature*, **176**, 745 (1955).

23. Barrer, R. M., *Nature*, **178**, 1410 (1956).

24. Barrer, R. M., and Brook, D., *Trans. Faraday Soc.*, **49**, 940 (1953).

25. Barrer, R. M., and Langley, D. A., *J. Chem. Soc.*, **1958**, 3804, 3811, 3817.

26. Barrer, R. M., and Meier, W. M., *Helv. Phys. Acta*, **29**, 229 (1956).

27. Barrer, R. M., and Stuart, W. I., *Proc. Roy. Soc. (London)*, **A243**, 172 (1957).

28. Bauer, R., and Schwarzenbach, G., *Helv. Chim. Acta*, **43**, 842 (1960).

29. Bengen, F., German Patent Application 12438 (Mar. 18, 1940); I. G. Farbenindustrie, German Patent 869,070 (Mar. 2, 1953); *C.A.*, P **48**, 11479c.

30. Bengen, F., U.S. Tech. Mission Film No. 6, Item II-7, German Patent Application O.A. 12438 (Mar. 18, 1940).

31. Bengen, F., *Angew. Chem.*, **63**, 207 (1951).

32. Bengen, F., and Schlenk, W., Jr., *Experientia*, **5**, 200 (1949); *C.A.*, **44**, 1910b (1950).

33. Bernal, J. D., *Discussions Faraday Soc.*, **25**, 7 (1958).

34. Borchert, W., *Z. Naturforsch.*, **3b**, 464 (1948).

35. Borchert, W., *Heidelberger Beitr. Mineral. u. Petrog.*, **3**, (2), 124 (1952).

*36. Branch, R. F., *Can. Chem. Processing*, **40**, (11), 105 (1956); (12), 80 (1956).

37. Breck, D. W., and Smith, J. V., *Sci. American*, **200**, 85 (1959).

38. Brit. Oxygen Co. Ltd. and Powell, H. M., British Patent 678,312 (Sept. 3, 1952); *C.A.*, **47**, 3532a (1953).

39. Broser, W., and Lautsch, W., *Z. Naturforsch.*, **8b,** 711 (1953).

*40. Caglioti, V., *Accad. naz. Lincei*, Varenna 7–22 (Aug. 1956).

41. Caglioti, V., and Giacomello, G., *Gazz. chim. ital.*, **69,** 245 (1939); *Ricerca sci.*, **10,** 271 (1939).

42. Caglioti, V., and Giacomello, G., "Consiglio Nazionale Delle Ricerche, Rome, 1958."

43. Caglioti, V., Liguori, A. M., Gallo, N., Giglio, E., and Scrocco, M., *J. Inorg. and Nuclear Chem.*, **8,** 572 (1958).

44. Calvin, M., Tollin, G., and Sogo, P. B., *J. chim. phys.*, **55,** 869 (1958).

45. Campbell, D., and Bulman, N., *Fortschr. Chem. org. Naturstoffe*, **9,** 443 (1952).

46. Caspari, W. A., *J. Chem. Soc.*, **1926,** 2944.

47. Caspari, W. A., *J. Chem. Soc.*, **1927,** 1093.

48. Cavalieri, L. F., Angelos, A., and Bolis, M. E., *J. Am. Chem. Soc.*, **73,** 4902 (1951).

49. Chleck, D. J., and Ziegler, C. A., *Nucleonics*, **17,** (9), 130 (1959).

50. Chleck, D. J., and Ziegler, C. A., *Intern. J. Appl. Radiation and Isotopes*, **7,** 141 (1959).

51. Christian, C. G., U.S. Patent 2,774,802 (Dec. 18, 1956).

52. Clapp, Leallyn B., Ch. 17, "The Chemistry of the Coordination Compounds," ed. John C. Bailar, Jr., New York, Reinhold Publishing Corp., 1956.

53. Clasen, H., *Z. Elektrochem.*, **60,** 982 (1956).

54. Claussen, W. F., *J. Chem. Phys.*, **19,** 259, 662, 1425 (1951).

55. Clemm, A., *Ann.*, **110,** 357 (1859).

56. Cooke, A. H., and Duffus, H. J., *Proc. Phys. Soc. (London)*, **67A,** 525 (1954).

57. Cooke, A. H., Meyer, H., Wolf, W. P., Evans, D. F., and Richards, R. E., *Proc. Roy. Soc. (London)*, **A225,** 112 (1954).

58. Cramer, F., "Einschlussverbindunger," Heidelberg, J. Springer-Verlag, 1954.

*59. Cramer, F., *Revs. Pure and Appl. Chem. (Australia)*, **5,** 143 (1955).

60. Cramer, F., "Proc. Intern. Conf. on Coord. Compounds, Amsterdam, 1955," p. 395.

61. Cramer, F., *Ber.*, **84,** 851, 855 (1951).

62. Cramer, F., *Ber.*, **86,** 1576 (1953).

63. Cramer, F., *Ber.*, **86,** 1582 (1953).

64. Cramer, F., *Angew. Chem.*, **68,** 115 (1956).

65. Cramer, F., *Angew. Chem.*, **64,** 136 (1952).

*66. Cramer, F., *Angew. Chem.*, **64,** 437 (1952).

67. Cramer, F., and Dietsche, W., *Chemistry & Industry (London)*, **1958,** 892.

68. Cramer, F., and Dietsche, W., *Chem. Ber.*, **92,** 378 (1959).

69. Cramer, F., and Dietsche, W., *Chem. Ber.*, **92,** 1739 (1959).

70. Cramer, F., and Elschnig, G. H., *Chem. Ber.*, **89,** 1 (1956).

71. Cramer, F., and Henglein, F. M., *Angew. Chem.*, **68,** 649 (1956).

72. Cramer, F., and Henglein, F. M., *Chem. Ber.*, **90,** 2561, 2572 (1957).

73. Cramer, F., and Henglein, F. M., *Chem. Ber.*, **91,** 308 (1958).

74. Cramer, F., and Windel, H., *Chem. Ber.*, **89,** 354 (1956).

*75. Croft, R. C., *Quart. Revs. (London)*, **14,** (1), 1 (1960).

76. Dacey, J. R., Smelko, J. F., and Young, D. M., *J. Phys. Chem.*, **59,** 1058 (1955).

77. Dalgliesh, C. E., *J. Chem. Soc.*, **1952,** 3940.

78. Davy, H., *Ann. chim.*, **79,** 26 (1811).

79. Deaton, W. M., *Gas*, **12,** 20, 58 (1936).

80. Deaton, W. M., and Frost, E. M., "U.S. Bureau of Mines Monograph, No. 8" (1949).

81. Dianin, A. P., *J. Russ. Phys. Chem. Soc.*, **46,** 1310 (1914); *C. A.*, **9,** 1903 (1915) and *Chem. Zentr.*, **I,** 1063 (1915).

82. Dietrich, H. von, and Cramer, F., *Ber.*, **87,** 806 (1954).

83. Doty, P., *Proc. Natl. Acad. Sci. U.S.*, **46,** 461 (1960).

84. Donath, W. A., U.S. Patent 2,904,511 (Sept. 15, 1959).

85. Dryden, J. S., and Meakins, R. J., *Nature*, **169,** 324 (1952).

86. Eley, D. D., *Research (London)*, **12,** 293 (1959).

87. Evans, R. E., Ormrod, O., Goalby, B. B., and Staveley, L. A. K., *J. Chem. Soc.*, **1950,** 3346.

88. Evans, D. F., and Richards, R. E., *J. Chem. Soc.*, **1952**, 3295, 3932.

89. Evans, D. F., and Richards, R. E., *Proc. Roy. Soc.*, (*London*), **A223**, 238 (1954).

90. Evans, D. F., and Richards, R. E., *Nature*, **170**, 246 (1952).

91. Faraday, M., *Quart. J. Sci.*, **15**, 71 (1823).

92. Ferguson, Lloyd, N., "Electron Structures of Organic Molecules," New York, Prentice-Hall, Inc., 1952.

93. Fernández-Morán, Humberto, "Fast Fundamental Transfer Processes in Aqueous Biomolecular Systems," p. 33, Dept. of Biol., Cambridge, Massachusetts Institute of Technology, 1960.

94. Ferroni, Enzo, and Cocchi, Marco, *Ann. chim.* (*Rome*), **48**, 630 (1958).

95. Fetterly, L. C., U.S. Patent 2,499,820 (Mar. 7, 1950).

96. Feughelman, M., Langridge, R., Seeds, W. E., Stokes, A.R., Wilson, H. R., Hooper, C. W., and Wilkins, M. H. F., *Nature*, **175**, 834 (1955).

97. Fieser, L. F., and Newman, M. S., *J. Am. Chem. Soc.*, **57**, 1602 (1935).

98. Forcrand, R. de, *Ann. chim.*, **7**, 384 (1903); *Compt. rend.* **134**, 835, 991 (1902); **135**, 959 (1902); **176**, 355 (1923); **181**, 15 (1925).

99. Franklin, R. E., Klug, A., Finch, J. T., and Holmes, K. C., *Discussions Faraday Soc.*, **25**, 197 (1958).

100. French, D., Levine, M. L., Pazur, J. H., and Norberg, E., *J. Am. Chem. Soc.*, **71**, 353 (1949).

101. Fresco, J. R., *Trans. N. Y. Acad. Sci.*, Series II, **21**, 653 (1959).

102. Fresco, J. R., and Alberts, B. M., *Proc. Natl. Acad. Sci. U.S.*, **46**, 311 (1960); *Chem. Eng. News*, **38**, (15), 56 (1960).

103. Fresco, J. R., and Doty, P., *J. Am. Chem. Soc.*, **79**, 3928 (1957).

104. Freundenberg, K., and Cramer, F., *Z. Naturforsch.*, **3b**, 464 (1948).

105. Freundenberg, K., and Cramer, F., *Ber.*, **83**, 296 (1950).

106. Freundenberg, K., and Jacobi, R., *Ann. Chem.*, **518,** 102 (1935).
107. Frost, E. M., and Deaton, W. M., *Proc. Natl. Gas Dept.*, AGA (1946).
108. Fuller, W., *J. Mol. Biol.*, **3,** 175 (1961).
109. Gallo, N., Giglio, E., and Liguori, A. M., *Ricerca sci.*, **28,** 173 (1958).
110. Gilreath, E. S., "Fundamental Concepts of Inorganic Compounds," pp. 203, 217, 219, New York, McGraw-Hill Book Co., Inc., 1958.
111. Gilson, D. F. R., and McDowell, C. A., *Nature*, **183,** 1183 (1959).
112. Go, Y., and Kratky, O., *Z. physik. Chem.*, **B26,** 439 (1934).
113. Godchat, M., Cauquil, G., and Calas, R., *Compt. rend.*, **202,** 759 (1936).
114. Gomberg, M., and Cone, L. H., *Ann.*, **376,** 183 (1910).
115. Gorin, M. H., and Rosenstein, L., U.S., Patent 2,774,752 (Dec. 18, 1956).
116. Gottschalk, A., *Revs. Pure and Appl. Chem. (Australia)*, **3,** 179 (1953).
117. Hart, M. I., Jr., and Smith, N. O., "Abstracts of Papers," 138th Meeting, Am. Chem. Soc., New York, p. 33S, Sept. 1960.
118. Hartley, E. G. J., *J. Chem. Soc.*, **97,** 1725 (1910).
119. Hayes, C. H., unpublished paper, "Inclusion Complexes and Optical Isomerism," 1960.
120. Haurowitz, F., *J. Am. Chem. Soc.*, **74,** 2266 (1952).
121. Henning, G. R., "Interstitial Compounds of Graphite," p. 125 in "Progress in Inorganic Chemistry," Vol. I, N. Y., Interscience Press, Inc., 1959.
122. Hertl, E., and Römer, G. H., *Ber.*, **63B,** 2446 (1930).
123. Hexter, R. M., and Goldfarb, T. D., *J. Inorg. and Nuclear Chem.*, **4,** 171 (1957).
124. Hofmann, K. A., and Arnoldi, H., *Ber.*, **39,** 339 (1906).
125. Hofmann, K. A., and Höchtlen, F., *Ber.*, **36,** 1149 (1903).

126. Hofmann, K. A., and Küspert, F., *Z. anorg. u. allgem. Chem.*, **15,** 204 (1897).

127. Holman, R. T., and Ener, Siret, *J. Nutrition.* **53,** 461 (1954).

128. Hommel, C., Chleck, D., Ziegler, C., and Brousaides, F., Preprint No. 4-SF60, Instrument Soc. of America, May, 1960.

129. Hückel, W. (Rathmann, F. H., translator), "Theoretical Principles of Organic Chemistry," 7th German ed., Vol. I, p. 166, Houston, Elsevier Pub. Co., 1955.

130. Hunter, R. F., Morton, R. A., and Carpenter, A. T., *J. Chem. Soc.*, **1950,** 441.

131. Hutchison, A. J. L., U.S. Patent 2,410,583 (Nov. 5. 1946).

132. James, W. J., French, D., and Rundle, R. E., *Acta Cryst.*, **12,** 385 (1959).

133. Jeffrey, G. A., Feil, D., and McMullen, R., Paper Presented at Am. Chem. Soc. Meeting, Div. of Phy. Chem., Seattle, Wash., 1960.

134. Jones, A. L., and Fay, P. S., U.S. Patent 2,732,418 (Jan. 24, 1956).

135. Keggin, J. K., and Miles, F. D., *Nature*, **137,** 577 (1936).

136. Kelley, Carl S., U.S. Patent 2,739,144 (Mar. 20, 1956).

137. Kemula, W., *Roczniki Chem.*, **26,** 261 (1952); *Prezemysl Chem.*, **33,** 453 (1954).

138. Kemula, W., and Sybilska, D., *Nature*, **185,** 237 (1960).

139. Ketelaar, J. A. A., "Chemical Constitution," 2nd ed. p. 363, New York, Elsevier Pub. Co., 1958.

140. Kingery, W. D., *Science*, **134,** 164 (1961).

141. Kitaigorodski, A. I., "Organicheskaya Kristallochimiya," Moscow: Acad. of Sciences, U.S.S.R. (1955).

142. Klotz, I., *J. Am. Chem. Soc.*, **68,** 2299 (1946).

143. Klotz, I. M., Burkhard, R. K., and Urquhart, J. M., *J. Am. Chem. Soc.*, **74,** 202, 209 (1952).

144. Kluiber, R. W., *J. Am. Chem. Soc.*, **82,** 4839 (1960).

*145. Kobe, K. A., and Domask, W. G., *Pet. Refiner*, **31,** (3), 106 (1952); (5), 151 (1952); (7), 125 (1952).

146. Kratky, O., and Giacomello, G., *Monatsh.*, **69,** 427 (1936).

147. Krebs, H., and Wagner, J. A., German Patent 1,013,657 (Aug. 14, 1957); *C.A.*, **54,** 329 (1960).

148. Krebs, H., and Diewald, J., German Patent 1,013,655 (Aug. 14, 1957); *C.A.*, **54,** 329 (1960).

149. Kuhn, R., and Sorensen, N., *Ber.*, **71,** 1879 (1939).

150. Lautsch, W. von, Wiemer, B., Zschenderlein, P., Kraege, H. J., Bandel, W., Günther, D., Schulz, G. and Gnichtel, H., *Kolloid-Z.*, **161,** 36 (1958).

151. Lautsch, W. von, Bandel, W., and Broser, W., *Z. Naturforsch.*, **11b,** 282 (1956).

152. Lautsch, W. von, Broser, W., Biedermann, W., and Gnichtel, H., *Angew. Chem.*, **66,** 123 (1954); *J. Polymer Sci.*, **17,** 479 (1955).

153. Lautsch, W. von, and Gunther, D., *Naturwiss.*, **44,** 492 (1957).

154. Lautsch, W. von, Rauhut, H., Grimm, W., and Broser, W., *Z. Naturforsch.*, **12b,** 307 (1957).

155. Lautsch, W. von, Wiechert, R., Gnichtel, H., Schuchardt, G., Kraege, H. J., Singewald, C., Broser, W., Becker, H., Rauhut, H., and Grimm, W., *Österr. Chemiker-Zgt.*, **58,** 33 (1957).

156. Lawton, D., and Powell, H. M., *J. Chem. Soc.*, **1958,** 2339.

157. Lederer, E., and Lederer, M., "Chromatography," New York, Elsevier Publishing Co., 1957.

158. Leicester, J., and Bradley, J. K., *Chemistry & Industry (London)*, **1955,** 1449.

159. Linstead, R. P., and Whalley, M. W., *J. Chem. Soc.*, **1950,** 2987.

160. Logan, A. V., and Carle, D. W., *J. Am. Chem. Soc.*, **74,** 5224 (1952).

161. London, F., *Z. physik. Chem.*, **B,11,** 222 (1930).

162. Lynch, Chas. S., U.S. Patent 2,714,586 (Aug. 2, 1955).

*163. Mandelcorn, L., *Chem. Rev.*, **59,** 827 (1959).

√*164. Martinette, M., Sr., *J. Chem. Educ.*, **30,** 628 (1953).

√*165. Martinette, M., Sr., *The Science Teacher*, **27,** (5), 42 (1960).

166. Mason, R., *Nature*, **181,** 820 (1958).

167. McElroy, W. D., and Glass, B., "The Mechanism of Enzyme Action," p. 211, Baltimore, The Hopkins Press, 1954.

168. McMullan, R., and Jeffrey, J. A., *J. Chem. Phys.*, **31,** 1231 (1959).

169. Meyer, H., O'Brien, M. C. M., and Van Vleck, J. H., *Proc. Roy. Soc. (London)*, **A243,** 414 (1958).

170. Milgrom, J., *J. Phys. Chem.*, **63,** 1843 (1959).

171. Moeller, Therald, "Inorganic Chemistry," p. 227, New York, John Wiley & Sons, Inc., 1954.

*172. Montel, G., *Bull. soc. chim. France*, **1955,** 1013.

173. Mulliken, R. S., *J. Am. Chem. Soc.*, **72,** 600 (1950); **74,** 811 (1952).

174. Mulliken, R. S., "Proc. Intern. Conf. on Coordination Compounds, 1955, Amsterdam," p. 336.

175. Mylius, F., *Ber.*, **19,** 999 (1886).

176. Newman, M. S., "Steric Effects in Organic Chemistry," Ch. 10, New York, John Wiley & Sons, Inc., 1956.

177. Newman, A. C. D., and Powell, H. M., *J. Chem. Soc.*, **1952,** 3747.

178. Newey, H. A., Shokal, E. C., Mueller, A. C., Bradley, T. F., and Fetterly, L. C., *Ind. Eng. Chem.*, **42,** 2538 (1950).

179. Nikitin, B. A., *Z. anorg. u. allgem. Chem.*, **227,** 81 (1936).

180. Nikitin, B. A., *Compt. rend. acad. sci.*, U.S.S.R., **29,** 571 (1940).

181. Nikitin, B. A., *J. Gen. Chem. (U.S.S.R.)*, **9,** 1167 (1939).

182. Nikitin, B. A., *Bull. Acad. Sci. U.S.S.R.*, **1,** 39 (1940); *C.A.*, **35,** 3494 (1941).

183. Nikitin, B. A., and Kovalskaya, M. P., *Bull. Acad. Sci. U.S.S.R., Div. Chem. Sci.*, **1952,** 23 (in English).

184. Ogston, A. G., *Nature*, **162,** 963 (1948).

185. Orchin, M., *J. Org. Chem.*, **16,** 1165 (1951).

186. Palin, D. E., and Powell, H. M., *J. Chem. Soc.*, **1947,** 208.

187. Palin, D. E., and Powell, H. M., *J. Chem. Soc.*, **1948,** 571.

188. Palin, D. E., and Powell, H. M., *J. Chem. Soc.*, **1948,** 815.

189. Palin, D. E., and Powell, H. M., *Nature*, **156,** 334 (1945).

190. Parsonage, N. G., and Staveley, L. A. K., *Mol. Phys.*, **2,** 212 (1959).

191. Pauling, L., and Marsh, R. E., *Proc. Natl. Acad. Sci. U.S.*, **38**, 112 (1952).

191a. Pauling, L., *Science*, **134**, 15 (1961).

192. Perutz, M. F., *Trans. Faraday Soc.*, **42B**, 187 (1946).

193. Perutz, M. F., *Proc. Roy. Soc. (London)*, **A195**, 473 (1949).

194. Perutz, M. F., *Research*, **12**, 326 (1959).

195. Peyronel, G. and Barbieri, G., *J. Inorg. and Nuclear Chem.*, **8**, 582 (1958).

196. Pfeiffer, P., "Organische Molekülverbindungen," 2nd ed., in "Chemie in Einzeldarstellungen," Vol. 11, Stuttgart, 1927.

197. Platteeuw, J. C., *Rec. trav. chim.*, **77**, 403 (1958).

198. Platteuw, J. C., and Van der Waals, J. H., *Rec. trav. chim.*, **78**, 126 (1959).

199. Platteuw, J. C., and Van der Waals, J. H., *Mol. Phys.*, **1**, 91 (1958).

*200. Powell, H. M., *Endeavour*, **9**, 154 (1950).

201. Powell, H. M., *Endeavour*, **15**, 20 (1956).

202. Powell, H. M., "Instituts Solvay, Brussels. Institut International de Chemie Dixiéme Conseil de Chemie, 1956" p. 193.

203. Powell, H. M., *J. Chem. Soc.*, **1948**, 619.

204. Powell, H. M., *J. Chem. Soc.*, **1948**, 61.

205. Powell, H. M., *J. Chem. Soc.*, **1948**, 571.

206. Powell, H. M., *J. Chem. Soc.*, **1948**, 815.

207. Powell, H. M., *J. Chem. Soc.*, **1950**, 298.

208. Powell, H. M., *J. Chem. Soc.*, **1950**, 300.

209. Powell, H. M., *J. Chem. Soc.*, **1950**, 468.

*210. Powell, H. M., *J. Chem. Soc.*, **1954**, 2658.

211. Powell, H. M., *J. Inorg. and Nuclear Chem.*, **8**, 546 (1958).

212. Powell, H. M., *Nature*, **168**, 11 (1951).

213. Powell, H. M., *Nature*, **170**, 155 (1952).

214. Powell, H. M., *Nature*, **176**, 1188 (1955).

215. Powell, H. M., *Rec. trav. chim.*, **75**, 1 (1955).

*216. Powell, H. M., *Rec. trav. chim.*, **75**, 885 (1956).

217. Powell, H. M., "Proc. Symposium on Coordination Chem., Copenhagen, 1953," p. 36.

218. Powell, H. M., *Research (London)*, **1**, 353 (1948).

219. Powell, H. M., *The Times, Science Rev.* (*London*), p. 4, (1958).

*220. Powell, H. M., "Weekly Evening Meeting," Roy. Soc. (London), Apr. 27, 1951.

221. Powell, H. M., and Bartindale, G. W. R., *J. Chem. Soc.*, **1945,** 799.

222. Powell, H. M., and Guter, M., *Nature*, **164,** 240 (1949).

223. Powell, H. M., and Huse, G., *J. Chem. Soc.*, **1943,** 435.

224. Powell, H. M., Huse, G., and Cooke, P. W., *J. Chem. Soc.*, **1943,** 153.

225. Powell, H. M., and Rayner, J. H., *Nature*, **163,** 566 (1949).

226. Powell, H. M., and Riesz, P., *Nature*, **161,** 52 (1948).

227. Powell, H. M., and Wetters, B. D. P., *Chemistry & Industry* (*London*), **1955,** 256.

228. Radzitsky, P. de, and Hanotier, J., "Abstracts of Papers," p. 4Q, 139th Meeting, Am. Chem. Soc., St. Louis, Mo., Mar. 1961.

229. Radzitsky, P. de, and Hanotier, J., private communication.

230. Rapson, W. S., Saunder, D. H., and Stewart, E. T., *J. Chem. Soc.*, **1946,** 1110.

231. Rapson, W. S., Saunder, D. H., and Stewart, E. T., *Proc. Roy. Soc.* (*London*), **A188,** 31 (1946); **A190,** 508 (1947).

232. Rayner, J. H., and Powell, H. M., *J. Chem. Soc.*, **1952,** 319.

233. Rayner, J. H., and Powell, H. M., *J. Chem. Soc.*, **1958,** 3412.

234. Redlich, O., Gable, P. M., Dunlop, A. K., and Miller, R. W., *J. Am. Chem. Soc.*, **72,** 4153 (1950).

235. Redlich, O., Gable, C. M., Beason, L. R., and Miller, R. W., *J. Am. Chem. Soc.*, **72,** 4161 (1950).

236. Redlich, O., Smith, A. E., Gable, C. M., Dunlop, A. K., and Miller, R. W., "Abstracts," p. 117, Amer. Chem. Soc. Meeting, Houston, Texas, Mar. 1950.

237. Robertson, John M., "Organic Crystals and Molecules," p. 246, Ithaca, New York, Cornell Univ. Press, 1953.

*238. Rüdorff, W., "Graphite Intercalation Compounds," p. 223 in "Advances in Inorganic Chemistry and Radiochemistry," Vol. I, New York, Academic Press, Inc., 1959.

*239. Rye, A., *Tidsskr. Kjemi. Bergvesen Met.*, **14**, 170 (1954); *C.A.*, **49**, 10204g (1954).

*240. Safford, E. L., unpublished paper, "Clathrate Compounds," 1961.

241. Saunder, D. H., *Proc. Roy. Soc. (London)*, **A190**, 508 (1947).

242. Schaeffer, W. D., U.S. Patent 2,769,851 (Nov. 6, 1956).

243. Schaeffer, W. D., Dorsey, W. S., and Christian, C. G., paper presented at Dec., 1957 meeting of the AAAS.

244. Schaeffer, W. D., Dorsey, W. S., and Christian, C. G., U.S. Patent 2,926,206 (Feb. 23, 1960).

245. Schaeffer, W. D., Dorsey, W. S., Skinner, D. S., and Christian, C. G., *J. Am. Chem. Soc.*, **79**, 5870 (1957).

246. Schaeffer, W. D., U.S. Patent 2,798,069 (July 2, 1957).

247. Schaeffer, W. D., and Dorsey, W. S., U.S. Patent 2,798,102 (July 2, 1957).

248. Schaeffer, W. D., and Wordie, J. D., U.S. Patent 2,798,103 (July 2, 1957).

249. Schaeffer, W. D., U.S. Patent 2,798,891 (July 9, 1957).

250. Schaeffer, W. D., McKinnis, A. C., and Dorsey, W. S., U.S. Patent 2,849,511 (Aug. 26, 1958).

251. Schaeffer, W. D., U.S. Patent 2,849,513 (Aug. 26, 1958).

252. Schaeffer, W. D., U.S. Patent 2,876,226 (Mar. 3, 1959).

253. Schaeffer, W. D., U.S. Patent 2,876,227 (Mar, 3, 1959).

254. Schardinger, F., *Z. Untersuch. Nahr. u. Genussm.*, **6**, 874 (1903).

255. Schlenk, H., "Progress in the Chemistry of Fats and other Lipids," Vol. 2, p. 243, London Press, Ltd. 1954.

256. Schlenk, H., and Holman, R. T., *J. Am. Chem. Soc.*, **72**, 5001 (1950).

257. Schlenk, H., and Holman, R. T., *Science*, **112**, (2897), 19 (1950).

258. Schlenk, H., Sand, D. M., and Tillotson, J. A., *J. Am. Chem. Soc.*, **77**, 3587 (1955); U.S. Patent 2,827,452 (Mar. 18, (1958).

259. Schlenk, H., Tillotson, J. A., and Lamp, B. G., *J. Am. Chem. Soc.*, **77**, 5437 (1955).

260. Schlenk, W., Jr., *Ann. Chem.*, **565,** 204 (1949).

261. Schlenk, W., Jr., *Ann. Chem.*, **573,** 142 (1951).

262. Schlenk, W., Jr., *Experientia*, **8,** 337 (1952).

*263. Schlenk, W., Jr., *Fortschr. chem. Forsch.*, **2,** 92 (1951).

264. Schlenk, W., Jr., *Svensk Kem. Tidskr.*, **67,** 435 (1955).

265. Schmidlin, J., and Lang, R., *Ber.*, **43,** 2817 (1910).

266. Schoch, T., *Advances in Carbohydrate Chem.*, **1,** 247, New York, Academic Press, Inc., 1945.

267. Schwarz, R., "The Chemistry of the Inorganic Complex Compounds," New York, John Wiley & Sons, Inc., 1923.

268. Seidell, A., "Solubilities of Inorg. and Metal Organic Compounds," 3rd ed., New York, D. Van Nostrand Company, Inc., 1940.

269. Sen Gupta, A., and Aggarwal, J. S., *J. Sci. Ind. Research (India)*, **15B,** 473 (1956).

270. Smith, A. E., *J. Chem. Phys.*, **18,** 150 (1950).

271. Smith, A. E., *Acta Cryst.*, **5,** 224 (1952).

272. Smith, A. E., Am. Chem. Soc., Div. Petrol. Chem. Symposium No. 33, 5 (1955).

273. Smith, A. E., Feldman, A. W., and Stone, G. M., U.S. Patent 2,736,647 (Feb. 28, 1956).

*274. Smith, J. W., *Science Progr.*, **36,** 664 (1948).

*275. Smith, J. W., *Science Progr.*, **38,** 698 (1950).

276. Sobotka, H., *Chem. Revs.*, **15,** 358 (1934).

277. Sobotka, H., and Goldberg, A., *Biochem. J.*, **26,** 905 (1932).

278. Stackelberg, M. von, *Naturwiss.*, **36,** 327 (1949); **38,** 456 (1951).

279. Stackelberg, M. von, *Rec. trav. chim.*, **75,** 902 (1956).

280. Stackelberg, M. von, "Proc. Inter. Conf. on Coordination Compounds, Amsterdam, 1955," p. 408.

281. Stackelberg, M. von, and Fruhbuss, H., *Z. Elektrochem.*, **58,** 99 (1954).

282. Stackelberg, M. von, Hoverath, A., and Scheringer, C., *Z. Elektrochem.*, **62,** 129 (1958).

283. Stackelberg, M. von, and Jahns, W., *Z. Elektrochem.*, **58,** 162 (1954).

284. Stackelberg, M. von, and Meinhold, W., Z. Elektrochem., **58,** 40 (1954).

285. Stackelberg, M. von, and Meuthen, B., Z. Elektrochem., **62,** 130 (1958).

286. Stackelberg, M. von, and Müller, H. R., Z. Elektrochem., **58,** 25 (1954).

287. Stackelberg, M. von, and Müller, H. R., J. Chem. Phys., **19,** 1319 (1951).

288. Staveley, L. A. K., J. Phys. Chem. Solids, **18,** 46 (1961).

289. Stetter, H. and Roos, E. E., Ber., **88,** 1390 (1955).

290. Takemura, K. H., Cameron, M. D., and Newman, M. S., J. Am. Chem. Soc., **75,** 3280 (1953).

291. Taylor, W. H., Z. Krist., **74,** 1 (1930).

292. Terres, E., and Thewait, K., Brennstoff-Chem., **38,** 257 (1957).

293. Terres, E., and Vollmer, W., Petroleum Z., **31,** (19), 1 (1935).

294. The Fluor Corp., Ltd., British Patents 568,290 and 568,292 (Mar. 28, 1945).

295. Truter, E. V., J. Chem. Soc., **1951,** 2416.

296. Ulmann, M., and Schierbaum, F., Kolloid-Z., **156,** 156 (1958).

297. Van der Waals, J. H., J. Phys. Chem. Solids, **18,** 82 (1961).

298. Van der Waals, J. H., Trans. Faraday Soc., **52,** 184 (1956).

299. Van der Waals, J. H., and Platteeuw, J. C., "Advances in Chemical Physics," ed. by I. Prigogine, Vol. 2, p. 1, London, Interscience Press, Inc., 1959.

300. Van der Waals, J. H., and Platteeuw, J. C., Nature, **183,** 462 (1959).

301. Vaughan, P., and Donahue, J., Acta Cryst., **5,** 570 (1952).

302. Verrijn-Stuart, A. A., "Proc. Intern. Conf. on Coordination Compounds, Amsterdam, 1955," p. 412.

303. Villard, P., Compt. rend., **123,** 377 (1896).

304. Waller, J. G., Nature, **186,** 429 (1960).

305. Wallwork, S. G., and Powell, H. M., J. Chem. Soc., **1956** 4855.

306. Weedman, John A., U.S. Patent 2,735,843 (Feb. 21, 1956).

307. Weiss, J., J. Chem. Soc., **1942,** 245.

308. Weiss, A., and Hofmann, U., Z. Naturforsch., **6b,** 405 (1951); **7b,** 363 (1952).

309. Wheland, C. W., "Advanced Organic Chemistry," 3rd ed., p. 155, New York, John Wiley & Sons, Inc., 1960.

310. Wieland, H., and Sorge, H., Z. physiol. Chem., **97,** 1 (1916).

311. Wilcox, W. I., Carson, D. B., and Katz, D. L., Ind. Eng. Chem., **33,** 662 (1941).

312. Williams, F. V., J. Am. Chem. Soc., **79,** 5876 (1957).

313. Windaus, A., Klänhard, F., and Weinhold, R., Z. physiol. Chem., **126,** 308 (1923).

314. Wohler, F., Ann., **69,** 294 (1849).

315. Wolf, A. P., Redvanly, C. S., and Anderson, R. C., Nature, **176,** 831 (1955).

316. Wynne-Jones, W. F. K., and Anderson, A. R., Compt. rend. 2e Réunion de chimie physique, Paris, p. 246, 1952.

*317. Zilberstein, G., Bull. soc. chim. France, **18,** D33 (1951).

318. Zimmerscheid, W. J., Higley, W. S., and Lien, A. P., Petroleum Eng. Reference Annual. C-43-7 (1950).

319. Zimmerscheid, W. J., Dinerstein, R. A., Weitkamp, A. W., and Marschner, R. F., Ind. Eng. Chem., **42,** 1300 (1950).

Index

Complex compounds
 conditions favoring formation of, 39, 41, 43
 definition, 1
Copper(II) inorganic complex
  compounds which form
  clathrates, 67
Cortisone, 144
Coumarin-I_2 compounds, 26
Covalent bonds in cage structures, 41–43
Cyanide complexes with metal-
  cyanide-metal structures,
  40
Cyclodextrins, 21
 gas complexes, 73
 guest molecules in, 131
 selective inclusion of, 131
 with iodine, 26
Cycloveratril clathrates, 57
 guest molecules in, 59
 infrared spectra, 90
 preparation of, 130
 structure, 58
Cymene clathrates, separation
  of isomers, 109, 163

Decompositions within the
  clathrate cage, 118
Deoxyribonucleic acid (DNA),
  an inclusion compound,
  159
Desoxycholic acid, 16, 144
Dextrin, α, β, γ, 21
Dianin's compound
 formulas, 68, 71
 guest components in, 71, 138
 preparation of addition compounds of, 136
 structure, 68

Dichlorobenzene, selective
  clathration of, 113
Dichlorobenzenes, separation of
  isomers of, 104, 110
Diethylbenzene, separation of
  isomers of, 109
Digitonin, 144
2, 2'-Dihydroxy-5, 5'-dimethyl-
  diphenylmethane clath-
  rate, preparation of, 137
Dimethoxybenzene clathrates,
  107
Dimethylnaphthalene clathrates, 107
4, 4'-Dinitrodiphenyl with 4
  hydroxydiphenyl clath-
  rates, 72
Dissociation reaction, 44
Double hydrates
 formulas and composition,
  101
 preparation, 127
Dyeing, 27

Encirclement formulas
 application, 48
 definition, 45
Energies of interaction of gas
  host molecules, with hydroquinone cage, 98
Enzyme action, inclusion in,
  157
Epitaxy studies of clathrates,
  116
Ethane-water clathrates, 127
Ethylbenzene, separation of
  from aromatic hydrocar-
  bon isomers, 106
Ethylene dichloride, as guest
  molecule, 71